kappa kappa gamma

An Introduction to Business

Learning business concepts through a simulation experience

Designed to accompany the Foundation™ 2006 simulation

University of Oregon
Lundquist College of Business
Dave Dusseau, Ph.D.
Doug Wilson, MBA

This material was developed by:
David Dusseau, Ph.D.
Doug Wilson, MBA
University of Oregon
Lundquist College of Business
Eugene, Oregon   97403-1208

541 346-3293
douglw@uoregon.edu

Foundation™ is a trademark of Management Simulations, Inc.™ and was developed by:
Management Simulations, Inc.
540 Frontage Road, Suite 3270
Northfield, Illinois   60039

847-501-2888
www.capsim.com

Table of Contents

A Prologue

The jobs most people have relate to business. No matter what your major, what area your degree or what career you choose, you will probably find yourself working in some type of a business setting. In addition to traditional business positions, the artist sells their work, the physician is employed by a hospital, the architect manages their firm and the non-profit pays their expenses — it all relates back to business.

This course is designed to provide a framework for understanding the essential aspects of business. The experience will demonstrate how the private enterprise system and businesses that participate in that system provide value for customers, clients and society through the products and services they offer.

The structure of this class offers an overview of business concepts by presenting information about business in conjunction with an online simulation. This simulation places *you* in the position of making business decisions for *your* company. A series of decisions you will make will enable you to see the outcome of your business choices in a competitive marketplace. The simulation requires you to establish your strategy, position your product, determine how you will promote your products, create a sales forecast, set inventory levels, and make a variety of other decisions that most businesses need to consider.

The objective of this experience is to offer an interactive and interesting way to learn about business, its terminology and concepts. The combination of the material you will be exploring along with the simulation may prove to better enable you to understand and appreciate the role business plays in our economic system, our society and each of our lives.

An Introduction to Business

Chapter 1

Private Enterprise: An economic system

The private enterprise system seeks to find and create opportunity through individuals acting in their own self interest as they direct resources and compete to create and keep their profits.

Key terms to look for:

- Demand
- Economic costs
- Economics
- Innovation
- Markets
- Opportunity costs
- Specialization
- Supply

Private Enterprise: An economic system

Resources are required to produce the goods and services that we need to survive and thrive in our environment. In the most basic sense, there are three kinds of resources required to produce these goods and services. These are called the factors of production and include:
- Raw materials *or natural resources;*
- Tools and machinery *or capital,* and;
- Labor *or human resources.*

Our desire for goods and services is based on our wants and, in many cases, those desires are greater than the resources available to satisfy them. This scarcity of resources requires that we make choices as to how these resources are to be used.

Dictionary.com defines the term **economics** as:

> "a social science that deals with the production, distribution, and consumption of goods and services and with the theory and management of economies or economic systems."

Therefore, economics is a study of how resources are distributed for the production of goods and services within a social system. All economic systems address the same basic set of questions:
- What goods and services and how much of each will be produced?
- How will the goods and services be produced, who will produce them, and with what resources?
- How will the goods and services be distributed?

Communism, socialism, and capitalism are different ways in which the economic system can be structured and organized. In a capitalist, or **private enterprise system**, individual citizens own and operate the majority of businesses and it is the market that determines the distribution of resources. Individuals act in their own self-interest and compete to participate in transactions in the markets available to them. The terms of the transaction, or the quantity traded and the trading price, is determined by the supply of and demand for that particular good.

Demand is the quantity of goods and services consumers are willing to buy at different prices. **Supply** is the quantity of goods and services businesses are willing to provide at those prices. Self-interest and competition will produce an efficient allocation of resources. Goods and services are desired and used where they produce the greatest benefit or are most productively used. Throughout this process, pressure is exerted from several aspects. For example, there is pressure to lower prices and pressure to innovate through technological and procedural improvements.

This system requires the existence of four characteristics:
1. Private property;
2. Freedom of choice;
3. The right to keep profits, and;
4. An environment where fair competition can occur.

Governments establish the economic system through the rule of law and also act to correct failures of the system.

Back in the U.S.S.R.

"We want a *voluntary* union of nations—a union which precludes any coercion of one nation by another—a union founded on complete confidence, on a clear recognition of brotherly unity, on absolutely voluntary consent." Lenin's words expressed a concept behind what became known as the U.S.S.R. The economic implications of this system evolved into a government that would determine what, how, and at what volume most goods and services would be produced and distributed. As if falling under its own weight, the former superpower and communist totalitarian state collapsed in December of 1991. After surviving for more than 70 years, the economic system of the U.S.S.R. failed.

Markets

The historical creation of markets involved actual markets where there were physical places designated for potential buyers and sellers to come in contact with one another to buy and sell goods. Today, we consider markets as any mechanism that facilitates the exchange of goods and services between buyers and sellers. The grocery store is a market where food is purchased, NASDAQ is an electronic market where buyers and sellers of stock come in contact, and the Internet enables online stores and trading sites to function. From a village square to eBay, markets have come a long way.

Markets are both specialized and complex. Consider all of the separate activities that have to be precisely coordinated in order for you to buy breakfast at a local café. Farmers, truck drivers, grocery workers, warehouses, distribution centers, cooks, and waiters represent just a few of the functions and people whose efforts contributed to the production, processing, transportation, and distribution of your meal.

In an economic context, *specialization* is a measure of how broadly or narrowly defined the range of included activities are. A bicycle shop is a more specialized retail store than Wal-Mart because the bicycle shop focuses on a narrow and deep range of products. Specialization creates an opportunity for greater efficiency and increased productivity. The division of tasks that comes with specialization introduces a need for coordination between

5

those specialized tasks. These different levels of specialization and different kinds of coordinating mechanisms create a complex economic environment.

Markets are also characterized by **uncertainty** and **risk**. Uncertainty is not knowing what will happen—the unpredictability about the consequences of your choice—in a decision situation. The greater the uncertainty, the less you know about the results of a particular choice. Decision makers work to reduce uncertainty by compiling as much relevant information as possible about a decision situation. Risk is also associated with the consequences of choice and, therefore, risk is a measure of the significance of those decisions.

Consider flipping a coin. You cannot consistently predict when you flip a nickel whether it will land with the "head" or the "tail" side up. Not knowing which side will land facing up is a form of uncertainty. If you place a bet with a friend about which side will land facing up, the amount of the bet would be a measure of the risk. If you are of average wealth in the United States and bet a nickel, then the risk associated with the bet would be small. If you are in the same economic position and bet $100,000, the risk associated with the bet becomes larger.

> ### *Decision-making*
> *A process of defining problems and opportunities that merit attention, generating and evaluating alternative courses of action, and committing to the action that is most likely to produce the optimal result.*

Decision-making involves comparing the economic and opportunity rewards (benefits) and sacrifices (costs) involved in a course of action and committing to the one that best meets your goals. The objective is to make the parties involved "better off" than they were before the transaction took place. Typically, good decisions are commitments that help you accomplish your goals, however you define them. Business decisions primarily focus on gaining economic rewards. This refers back to the assumption that we only engage in transactions that offer the potential to improve our "position." When we choose a course of action, it requires a sacrifice to obtain the reward. In economic terms, this sacrifice is a "cost." A decision maker considers two kinds of costs, the economic cost and the opportunity cost, when evaluating alternative choices available.

1. The **economic cost** is the money spent implementing the decision.

2. The **opportunity cost** is the cost of what you gave up doing when you committed to the course of action you chose.

Consider the decision you made after graduating from high school. You basically had two choices:

1. You could have begun working immediately after high school and taken a job that pays $20,000 a year, or;

2. You could attend a college or university.

The *economic cost* of the college alternative is the cost of tuition, books, fees, and living expenses. The *opportunity cost* of the college alternative is the income that you gave up when you did *not* take the job. In the long run, opportunity costs are often more important than economic costs.

Business decisions consider economic and opportunity costs and provide a structure to make those decisions. Business does have its own vocabulary and there are terms that will be helpful to know. A few of these terms include the following:

- A **business** is an organization or individual that seeks a profit by providing products that satisfy people's needs (or wants).

- A **product** is a good, service, or idea that has both tangible and intangible characteristics that provide the satisfaction or benefits.

- **Profit**, the basic goal of business, is the difference between what it costs to make and sell a product and what the customer pays for it.

- **Stakeholders** are groups of people who have a vested interest ("stake") in the actions a business takes (decisions a business makes). There are four major groups of stakeholders — *owners, employees, customers, and citizens*. The specific interests of each of these stakeholder groups may conflict.

Activities of Business

The most basic way to categorize the activities of business falls into the areas of marketing, production, finance and accounting.

- **Marketing** refers to the activities designed to provide goods and services that satisfy customers. These activities include market research, development of products, pricing, promotion, and distribution.

- **Accounting** refers to the process that tracks, summarizes and analyzes a firm's financial position.

- **Production** refers to the activities and processes used in making products. Activities involve designing the production process (investments in facilities and equipment) and the efficient management and operation of those processes.

- **Finance** refers to the activities concerned with funding a business and using resources effectively.

Managing a Business

Decisions that shape the marketing, production, and financial functions are made in specialized, complex, uncertain, and risky market environments. Managing these functions requires planning, organizing, operating and controlling the various aspects of the business.

- *Planning:* Determining what the organization needs to do and how to get it done.

- *Organizing:* Arranging the organizations resources and activities in such a way as to make it possible to accomplish the plan

- *Operating:* Enacting the plan including guiding and motivating employees to work toward accomplishing the necessary tasks

- *Controlling:* Measuring performance, comparing performance to expectations established in the planning process, and adjusting either the performance or the plan.

In achieving the goals of the organization, managers need to be both ***effective*** and ***efficient***.

*****Effective*** *refers to doing the right thing.***

*****Efficient*** *refers to doing things right.***

Being effective involves committing to a course of action that will allow you to accomplish your goals. It is a measure of the "goodness" of the outcomes of your actions. Being efficient refers to employing an appropriate process to achieve your goals. Measures of efficiency involve comparing the resources invested to the outcomes that are achieved.

In Foundation™

The simulation that you will experience is called "Foundation." This web-based simulation will require you to apply each of these business concepts. You will address marketing, production, accounting and finance issues as you take over your company's production and sale of goods. You will need to plan, organize, operate and control the direction of your company as you compete for market share with other firms in this free enterprise environment. With less than perfect information, you must decide what volume of product to produce, how to promote your products, how to finance your expenses, and how to assess your financial performance. After each set of decisions, you will then receive your results based upon your ongoing performance in the market, the profitability of your firm, and the value you have provided your stockholders.

Foundation is a registered trademark of MSI

Competing in this private enterprise environment offers value for consumers. It offers additional choices and business are motivated to innovate often through technological advancements to improve their offerings and make them more attractive. It is through *innovation* and the motivation to price their products and services attractively to better position their business for future success.

Review and Discussion Questions

1. What set of questions do all economic systems address and why are those areas important?

2. What are the general activities of business and what roles do they play?

3. What best describes the concept of "scarcity?"

4. What does it mean to describe markets as "specialized?"

5. Provide examples of "opportunity costs" that are relevant to you taking this course.

6. What impact does the private enterprise system have on innovation?

7. Give an example of "uncertainty" and how it relates to risk and decision making.

Chapter 2

Marketing: Concept and application

Marketing is the process of planning and executing the conception, pricing, promotion and distribution of ideas, goods and services to create exchanges that satisfy individual and organizational objectives.

— American Marketing Association

Key terms to look for:

- Marketing mix
- Market research
- Marketing strategy
- Promotion
- Accessibility
- Sales forecasting
- Segmentation
- Target marketing

Marketing: Concept and Application

The Marketing Function
To be successful in a private enterprise system, you have to be able to entice people to trade with you. Remember, individuals will only trade goods and services *if* they are going to be "better off" as a result of the transaction. The essential questions become "who are those people?" and "how can you create value for them?" Marketing addresses these questions.

Marketing defines your strategy for competing in the marketplace. Managers need to understand and develop marketing programs to promote their products and services. Business success is based on the ability to build a growing body of satisfied customers. Marketing programs are built around the "marketing concept" and performance which directs managers to focus their efforts on identifying, satisfying and following up the customer's needs—all at a profit.

The Marketing Concept
The marketing concept focuses on the importance of customers to a firm and states that all company policies and activities should be aimed at satisfying customer needs. Realizing a profitable sales volume is better than maximizing sales volume at the cost of profitability.

To use the marketing concept, a business must understand how to accomplish the following:
- *Market Research* determines the needs of their customers
- *Market Strategy* analyze their competitive advantages, plans and actions
- *Target Marketing* selects specific markets to serve
- *Market Mix* determines how to satisfy those needs through addressing product, price, place, promotion and service

Market Research
To be successful, a business must know its market. Market research is simply an orderly and objective way of learning about people—the group of people who buy from you or have the highest propensity to do so. Market research is the systematic gathering, recording, and analyzing of data about problems relating to marketing goods and services.

Market research is not a perfect science. It deals with people and their constantly changing likes, dislikes and behaviors potentially affected by hundreds of influences.

Market research attempts to learn about markets scientifically and gather facts and opinions in an orderly and objective way. Market research seeks to find out how things are, not how you think they are or would like them to be. Market research attempts to find out what specific products or services people want to buy, rather than focusing on what you want to sell them.

Market research is an organized way of finding objective answers to questions every business must answer to succeed. Every small business owner-manager must ask:

- Who are my customers and potential customers?
- What kind of people are they?
- Where do they live?
- Can and will they buy from my business?
- Am I offering the kinds of goods or services they want at the best place, at the best time and in the right amounts?
- Are my prices consistent with what buyers view as the product's value?
- Are my promotional programs working by creating awareness in the market place?
- Are my sales programs working to create accessibility for my product through the distribution channel?
- What do customers think of my business?
- How does my business compare with my competitors?
- Are there specific reasons customers would make the decision to purchase from my business versus my competitors?

Reasons for Market Research

It is difficult, maybe even impossible, to sell people things that they do not want. Business managers have to view their business from a customer perspective. They combine this perspective with their sense of the market that comes from experience. But experience is not always a good thing. This experience may include a tremendous mass of information acquired at random over a number of years and some of that information may no longer be timely or relevant to making selling decisions. Some facts may be vague, misleading impressions or folk tales that may lead an organization in the wrong direction.

Market research focuses and organizes marketing information. It ensures that such information is timely. Sound market research provides what you need to:

- Reduce business risks.
- Identify problems and potential problems in your current market.
- Discover and profit from sales opportunities.
- Acquire facts about your market to develop a marketing strategy and implement action plans.
- Assist you in making better decisions and make corrections as needed.

Conducting Market Research

Many managers do some from of market research every day without being aware of it. In their daily managerial duties, they check returned items to see if there is some pattern. They run into one of your old customers and ask her why she has not been in lately. They look at a competitor's ad to see what that store is charging for the same products you are selling. These activities provide a framework that enables managers objectively judge the meaning of the information they gather about their market.

A more formal market research process includes these steps:
1. Define the problem or opportunity
2. Access available information
3. Gather additional information, if required
4. Review internal records and files; interview employees
5. Collect outside data (secondary and primary)
6. Organize and interpret data
7. Make a decision and take action
8. Assess the results of the action

Defining the Problem or Opportunity

Defining the problem or assessing the opportunity is the first step of the research process. This process is often overlooked, yet it is the most important step. You must be able to see beyond the symptoms of a problem to get at the cause. Seeing the problem as a sales decline is not defining a cause, it is merely listing a symptom.

You must establish an idea of the problem with causes that can be objectively measured and tested. Look at your list of possible causes frequently while you are gathering your facts, but do not let it get in the way of the facts. To define your problem, list every possible influence that may have caused it. Have your customers changed? Have their tastes changed? Have their buying habit changed? List the possible causes. If there are areas that cannot be tracked, realize that you may not be able to objectively measure your progress toward that goal.

Assessing Available Information

Once you have formally defined your problem, assess the information that is immediately available. You may already have all the information you need to determine if your hypothesis is correct, and solutions to the problem may have become obvious in the process of defining it. Stop there. You have reached a point of diminishing returns. You will be wasting time and money if you do further marketing research and do not gain additional insight.

If you are uncertain if you need additional information, you must weigh the cost of more information against its usefulness. You are up against a dilemma similar to guessing in advance of what return you will receive on your advertising dollar. You do not know what return you will get, or even if you will get a return. The best you can do is to balance that against the cost of gathering more data to make a better informed decision.

Gathering Additional Information

Begin by "thinking cheap and staying as close to home as possible." Before considering anything elaborate, such as surveys or field experiments, explore your own records and files. Look at sales records, complaints, receipts and any other records that can help you better understand you where your customers live, work, what they buy, and how they buy it.

For example, your customers' addresses can tell you a lot about them. You may be able to make guesses about their life-styles by knowing their neighborhoods. Knowing how they live can give you solid hints on what they can be expected to buy.

Credit records are an excellent source of information about your markets. In addition to customers' addresses, they give you information about their jobs, income levels and marital status. Offering credit is a multifaceted marketing tool, although one with well known costs and risks.

When you have finished checking through your records, turn to that other valuable internal source of customer information: your employees. Employees may be the best source of information about customer likes and dislikes. They hear customers' complaints about the store or service — often the ones the customers do not think are important enough to take to you as the owner-manager. Employees are aware of the items customers request that you may not stock. They can probably supply good customer profiles from their day-to-day contacts.

External Data

Once you have exhausted your internal sources for information about your market, the next steps in the process are to do primary and secondary research outside.

Secondary Research

Secondary research involves going to already published surveys, books, magazines and other resources and applying or rearranging the information in them to bear on your particular problem or potential opportunity.

For example:

> You sell tires. You might guess that sales of new cars three years ago would have a strong effect on present retail sales of tires. To test this idea you might compare new car sales of six years ago with replacement tire sales from three years ago.

> Suppose you found that new tire sales three years ago were 10 percent of the new car sales three years before that. Repeating this exercise with car sales five years ago and tire sales two years ago, and so on, you might find that in each case tire sales were about 10 percent of new car sales made three years before. You could then logically conclude that the total market for replacement tire sales in your area this year should be about 10 percent of new car sales in your locality three years ago.

Naturally, the more localized the figures you can find, the better. For instance, there may be a national decline in new housing starts, but if you sell new appliances in an area in which new housing is booming, you obviously would want to base your estimate of market potential on local conditions. Newspapers and local radio and television stations may be able to help you find this information.

There are many sources of secondary research material. You can find it in libraries, universities and colleges, trade and general business publications, and newspapers. Trade associations and government agencies are rich sources of information.

Primary Research

Primary research on the outside can be as simple as asking customers or suppliers how they feel about your store or service firm or as complex as the surveys conducted by sophisticated professional marketing research firms. Primary research includes among its tools direct mail questionnaires, telephone or on-the-street surveys, experiments, panel studies, test marketing, behavior observation and so on.

Primary research is often divided into reactive and non-reactive research. Non-reactive primary research is a way to see how real people behave in a real market situation without influencing that behavior. Reactive research, such as surveys, interviews, and questionnaires, is what most people think of when they hear the words marketing research. It is best left to the experts, as you may not know the right questions to ask. There's also the danger that people will answer questions the way they think they are expected to answer, rather than telling you how they really feel about your product, service or business.

Organizing and Interpreting Data

After collecting the data you must organize it into meaningful information. Go back to your definition of the problem, compare it with your findings and prioritize and rank the data.

- What strategies are suggested?
- How can they be accomplished?
- How are they different from what I am doing now?
- What current activities should be increased?
- What current activities must I drop or decrease in order to devote adequate resources to new strategies?

Making Decisions and Taking Action

Prioritize each possible strategy from the standpoint of :

- Immediate goal to be achieved
- Cost to implement
- Time to accomplish
- Measurement of success

For example, if your research suggested ten possible strategies, select two or three that appear to have the greatest impact potential or are most easily achievable and begin there. For each strategy, develop tactics that may include:

- Staff responsibilities
- Necessary steps
- Budget allocations
- Timelines with deadlines for accomplishing strategic steps
- Progress measurements

Based on this information, make a final decision on the strategies and go to work on the tactics.

16

Assessing the Results of the Action

Analyze your progress measures. If adjustments are appropriate, make them. At the conclusion of the time you have allotted for accomplishing your goal, take a hard look at the results.

- Did you achieve your goal?
- Should the decision be renewed on a larger scale?

If you are disappointed in the results, determine why the plan went awry.

The Possibilities

Market research is limited only by your imagination. You can conduct a significant amount of market research at very little cost except your time and mental effort. While large companies generally have and use a wealth of available data on many business problems, smaller companies often ignore such data because they are unaware of its existence, although it may be as close as next door. Here are a few examples of techniques small business owner-managers have used to gather information about their customers.

The local public, trade school, college or university library is a prime source of inexpensive, targeted information about business topics such as competition, the law, government, society, culture, economics and technology.

Although the resources of public libraries vary widely, the library's four walls and the size of its collection do not limit its service. New information technologies have changed libraries dramatically. Many academic libraries are open to the public. A typical library includes reference and general books, periodicals and possibly one or more specialized collections. Several tools and services help one find material.

Indexes help find information in leading magazines, journals or newspapers. Among these are the Business Index, the Business Periodical Index, the Public Affairs Information Service Bulletins (PAS), the Statistical Reference Index, the Wall Street Journal Index, and the American Statistics Index. These indexes list articles according to subject headings; they supply the title and author as well as the publication title, date and page number. Indexes are available in several formats including printed versions, optical disks, film, CD-ROMS (compact disk read-only memory) and on-line databases.

The Index to U.S. Government Periodicals is another sources and much of this information is accessible online. One example is information provided by the US Census bureau found at www.uscensus.gov.

Information about industries and individual companies can also be found under Standard Industrial Classification (SIC) headings. SIC is a uniform coding system developed by the federal government to classify establishments according to economic activity. Codes for specific industries are listed in the Standard Industrial Classification Manual. Four-digit codes define specific industries such as SIC 2653, corrugated and solid fiber box manufacturers, or SIC 5812, eating establishments. Most federal government economic data and many business and industrial directories use SIC codes.

In order to manage the marketing functions successfully, good information about the market is necessary. Frequently, a market research program can disclose problems and areas of dissatisfaction that can be easily remedied, or new products or services that could be offered successfully.

Market research should also encompass identifying trends that may affect sales and profitability levels. Population shifts, legal developments, and the local economic situation should be monitored to enable early identification of problems and opportunities. Competitor activity should also be monitored. Competitors may be entering or leaving the market, for example. It is also very useful to know what your competitors' strategies are (i.e., how they compete).

Marketing Strategy

Marketing strategy encompasses identifying customer groups, or target markets, which a small business can serve better than its competitors, and tailoring its product offerings, prices, distribution, promotional efforts and services towards that particular market segment. This may be referred to as "Managing the Market Mix." Ideally, the marketing strategy should address customer needs which currently are not being met in the market place and which represent adequate potential size and profitability. A good marketing strategy implies that a small business cannot be all things to all people and must analyze its market and its own capabilities. This provides a focus on a target market it can serve best and increases the effectiveness of marketing activities and provides a better return based on the use of the marketing budget.

Dell's Approach to Marketing

The lobby of one of Dell Computer's corporate offices has a huge sign that says "Think customer." This captures Dell's innovative way of understanding, reaching and serving customers. The direct-to-customer business model Dell has created allows customers to buy directly from the manufacturer. This direct connection with customers has enabled Dell to be highly responsive to meeting customer needs in a cost effective manner. This marketing channel has allowed Dell to price its products 10 to 15 percent under that of competitors. Dell takes delivery of components as needed with the ability to build a PC within eight hours of taking the order. This just-in-time production system is combined with a service concept based on "the Dell vision" that states that a customer "must have a quality experience and must be pleased, not just satisfied." Dell offers exceptional service and delivery, from single end-users to corporate accounts such as Boeing that purchase as many as 1,000 personal computers each week. Dell has demonstrated the power of its marketing channel combined with competitive pricing and a responsive service philosophy.

Target Marketing

Owners of small businesses have limited resources to spend on marketing activities. Concentrating their marketing efforts on one or a few key market segments is the basis of target marketing. The major ways to segment a market are:

Geographic segmentation — Focusing on understanding the needs of customers in a particular geographical area. For example, a neighborhood convenience store may send advertisements only to people living within one-half mile of the store.

Demographic segmentation — Focusing on the attributes of the market based upon gender, age, income, education or other measurable factors.

Psychographic segmentation — Identifying and promoting to groups of people based on lifestyle and behaviors that are most likely to buy the product. This may be based on interests, fears, behaviors and actions that can be categorized into groups.

Target marketing enables you to identify, access, communicate with, and sell to those that are most likely to purchase your products.

Managing the Market Mix

There are five key marketing decision areas in a marketing program and they include:
1. Products and Services
2. Promotion
3. Distribution
4. Pricing
5. Service

The marketing mix is used to describe how owner-managers combine these four areas into an overall marketing program.

Products and Services — Effective product strategies for a small business may include concentrating on a narrow product line, developing a highly specialized product or service or providing a product-service package containing an unusual amount of service.

Price — Determining price levels and/or pricing policies is the major factor affecting total revenue. This includes determining the credit policy: Will you allow your customer to pay for the product *after* they receive it, or do they need to pay for it *when* they receive it? In the most general sense, higher prices mean lower volume and lower prices mean higher volume. However, small businesses can often command higher prices because of the personalized service they offer. And there have been situations where higher prices are associated with higher quality, and increasing the price to a certain point, results in increased volume. Hair care products are one category where this has occurred.

Promotion — This set of marketing decisions includes leveraging the Internet, various forms of advertising, salesmanship and other promotional activities. Offering special financing or extended terms is another form of promotion. In general, effective promotional strategies are a must for businesses because of the cost of extensive advertising campaigns and the limitations this imposes.

Place or Distribution Channel — The manufacturer and wholesaler must decide how to distribute their products. Working through established distributors or manufacturers' agents generally is most feasible for small manufacturers. Small retailers should consider cost and traffic flow as two major factors in location site selection, especially since advertising and rent can be reciprocal. In other words, low-cost, low-traffic location means you must spend more on advertising to build traffic. Investing efforts to increase ***accessibility*** is a key factor in product distribution.

Service — This area is a relatively recent addition to the traditional four Ps — product, price, place and promotion — of the marketing mix. Customer service is another way that an organization can provide value and differentiate itself from others that offer similar or identical products. Organizations like Nordstrom, Lexus, Eddie Bauer and the Northwest's Les Schwab Tires have created highly successful businesses based on offering exceptional customer service.

The nature of the product or service also is important in location decisions. If purchases are made largely on an impulse basis, such as flavored popcorn, high traffic and visibility are critical. On the other hand, location is less a concern for more specialized products or services that customers are willing to go out of their way to find. The ability the Internet offers to reach highly segmented customers online has enabled many businesses to operate anywhere and serve local, national and international markets.

In Foundation™

You will have the opportunity to determine how much you spend on marketing observe its impact on your business. You will learn about the "low tech" and high tech" target markets, their preferences, the reasons they are most likely to buy your products, and how those change from year to year. A perceptual map will help you visualize how those preferences shift and progress in relation to your product's attributes. "Promotions" expenditures will impact the awareness your markets have about your product—does your target market know you exist? "Sales" expenditures will impact the distribution and availability of your product—does your target market have access to those products. You will also be able to compete based on the payment schedule you offer your customers. For example, your products may be more attractive if you allow your customers to pay in 60 days rather than in a 30-day time period. A part of the process will be to create a sales forecast. Creating the sales forecast may be one of the most challenging tasks of all as you attempt to predict your own performance along with that of your competitors.

The Sales Forecast

Another aspect of marketing is to create a sales forecast to attempt to predict your unit sales and revenue performance. The sales forecast process often begins by assessing how the total market will perform. From here, you may attempt to assess your performance and what market share it will realize from that total forecast. This requires you to speculate on how your competitors will perform as well. This is often a challenging task due to the multiple variables involved in the process.

- What will the overall economic climate be like?
- Will consumers make decisions on the same basis they have in the past?
- At what level will our competitors perform?
- Will they introduce new products and if so, when would that be expected?
- Will there be new competitors or will existing competitors drop out of the market?

These questions are difficult and considering the possible outcomes may provide insight into making better forecasting decisions.

Marketing Performance

After marketing program decisions are made, owner-managers need to evaluate how well decisions have turned out. Standards of performance need to be set up so results can be evaluated against them. Sound data on industry norms and past performance provide the basis for comparing against present performance. Owner-managers should audit their company's performance on a periodic basis, at least quarterly.

The key questions to ask are:

- Is the company doing all it can to be customer-oriented?

- Do the employees make sure the customer's needs are truly satisfied and leave them with the feeling that they would enjoy coming back?

- Is it easy for the customer to find what he or she wants and at a competitive price?

In Foundation™

Your marketing strategy will determine the price and the attributes of your products. This includes your product's performance, size, and reliability. You also have access to market research conducted on each of your target markets. This research is valuable to enable you to understand what is important to your customers. You will know range of what they are will to pay for your products and how they want that produce to perform. You also have to consider what products your competitors are offering — their prices and how their performance, size and reliability compares with yours. Your product awareness and accessibility are other factors that influence your sales volume. Your marketing strategy, shaped by how well you understand your potential customers, will play a significant role regarding how successful you are at accomplishing your business objectives.

Review and Discussion Questions

1. Define the term "market."

2. What is the primary function of the research and development department?

3. Give no less than four examples of forms of distribution.

4. What is the essential goal of market research?

5. What are the differences between awareness and accessibility?

6. What elements are involved in the marketing mix and how do they interact with each other?

7. What do perceptual maps offer that other data presentations may not?

8. What does distribution mean?

9. How has the Internet changed distribution and what markets or types of industries have been impacted the most?

10. What comprises a good marketing strategy?

11. Why is it important to track the impact of a promotional and sales budget and what can be learned from tracking this data over time?

Chapter 3

Accounting: A business information system

Accounting tracks, summarizes and reports business operations in a way to assist with performance assessment and better decision making for the future.

Key terms to look for:

- Assets
- Balance sheet
- Cash flow
- Contribution margin
- Dividend
- GAAP
- Gross margin
- Income statement
- Liabilities
- Owner's Equity
- Liquidity
- Net income
- Retained earnings

Accounting: A business information system

A company has a responsibility to their stakeholders — a diverse group of people with different needs from the company. This includes:

- Owners
- Employees
- Customers
- Citizens (and the government that represents their interests)
- Creditors and financial institutions

These groups use accounting information to determine the degree to which the company is meeting its responsibilities. Accounting provides a function that helps managers monitor the operations of the business and report their financial conditions to those inside and outside of the business. Managers can assess the performance of production, marketing and finance decisions and they may rely on accounting information to detect inefficient use of resources. Optimizing the use of resources — time, materials, and money — may result in greater efficiencies and therefore, generate greater earnings.

The accounting system of a business generates information about the economic consequences of a company's activities. It is the historical summary and analysis of an organization's financial condition. These activities are identified, measured, recorded, and retained and then communicated in a set of accounting reports, or statements. Management accounting provides vital information about a company to internal users; financial accounting gives information about a company to external users.

Management Accounting

Management accounting helps managers plan, operate, and control a company's activities. The information provided through management accounting gives people inside a company vital business information. Managers need information to help them compete in a world market in which technology and methods of production are constantly changing. Managers must manage data in a way that will let them use it more efficiently and effectively. Accounting is one of the critical tools of information management.

The management accounting system provides information for managers inside the company. It is free from the restrictions of outside regulation and can be expressed in the form that is most useful for managers. Information can be reported in dollars, units, hours worked, products manufactured, numbers of defective products, or the quantity of contracts signed. Management accounting has to produce information that is relevant to specific segments of the company, products, tasks, plants, or activities. The sole criterion for management accounting is to provide information that enables managers to make more informed and effective decisions.

Financial Accounting

Financial reports provide a source of information about the company's performance. Financial accounting involves the identification, measurement, recording, accumulation, and communication of economic information about a company for external users to apply to their decisions. External users are people and groups outside the company who need accounting information to decide whether or not to engage in some activity with the company. These users include individual investors, stockbrokers and financial analysts who offer investment assistance, consultants, bankers, suppliers, labor unions, customers, and local, state, and federal governments and governments of countries in which the company does business.

Generally Accepted Accounting Principles

Over the years, a set of broad guidelines for financial accounting has evolved within the United States called "Generally Accepted Accounting Principles" or GAAP. For these financial reports to be useful, companies must follow specific guidelines, or rules. These principles have been developed to ensure that information reported is relevant, reliable, material, and valid.

Generally accepted accounting principles are the currently recognized principles, procedures, and practices that are used for financial accounting in the United States. These principles, or "rules," must be followed in the external reports of all companies that sell stock to the public and by many other companies as well. GAAP cover such issues as how to account for inventory, buildings, income taxes, and capital stock, how to measure the results of a company's operations, and how to account for the operations of companies in specialized industries, such as banking, entertainment, and insurance industries. Many GAAP pronouncements are complex and technical in nature and these principles do change. They are modified as business practices and decisions change as the Internal Revenue Service (IRS) makes new ruling and as better accounting techniques are developed.

Without these agreed-upon principles, external users of accounting information would not be able to understand the meaning of this information. Accounting is the language of business decision making. You can think of GAAP as the agreed-upon rules of "spelling and grammar" for business communication. These rules provide a consistent basis of understanding and communicating about the financial aspects of business activities.

Management Activities

To help ensure the success of the company, managers use accounting information as they perform the activities of planning the operations of the company, operating the company, and controlling the operations of the company for future planning and operating decisions.

Planning

Management begins with planning. Planning establishes the company's goals and the means of achieving these goals. Managers use the planning process to identify what resources, such as technological, human, and material, the company needs to achieve its goals. They use the planning process to set standards or "benchmarks," against which they later can measure the company's progress toward its goals. By periodically measuring the company's progress against those standards, managers identify when and how the company needs to make adjustments. Because the business environment changes so rapidly, planning is an ongoing process and must be flexible enough to deal with change.

To be effective in the planning process, managers have to consider the characteristics of the environment external to the organization. This includes the economic system, the political climate, the relative health of the monetary system, and the strength of the markets in which they operate. Managers must also create and communicate these plans in the social context of the organization. A plan is good only if everyone else believes in it. Accounting information plays an important role in capturing what has taken place to provide a basis on which to create a compelling and measurable view of the company's future.

Operating

Operating refers to the set of activities that enable the company to conduct its business according to its plan. A company's operating activities ensure that products or services get made and sold as planned and on schedule. This involves gathering the resources and employees necessary to achieve the goals of the company, establishing organizational relationships among departments and employees, and working toward achieving the goals of the company.

In the process of operating a company, managers and work-teams must make day-to-day decisions about how best to achieve these goals. For example, accounting information gives them valuable data about a product's performance. With this information, they can decide which products to continue to sell and when to add new products or drop old ones. If the company is a manufacturing company, managers and work teams can decide what products to produce and whether there is a better way to produce them. Accounting information enables managers to also make decisions about how to establish product prices, whether to advertise and how much to spend on advertising, and whether to buy new equipment or expand facilities. These decisions are ongoing. The results and outcomes of these decisions are reviewed and that information is used to make the next set of decisions.

Controlling

Controlling is the management activity that measures actual operations against standards or benchmarks. It provides feedback for managers to correct deviations from those standards, and to plan for the company's future operations. Controlling is a continuous process that attempts to prevent problems and to detect and correct problems as quickly as possible. Planning, operating, and controlling all require information. The company's accounting system provides much of the quantitative information managers' use.

Accounting Support for Management Activities

Management accounting involves the identification, measurement, recording, accumulation, and communication of economic information about a company for internal users in management decision-making. Internal users include individual employees, work groups or teams, departmental supervisors, divisional and regional managers, and "top management." With the help of the management accountant, these internal users use this information to help them make more effective decisions.

The reports that result from management accounting may forecast revenues (amounts charged to customers), predict costs of planned activities, and provide a business analysis based on these forecasts. By describing how alternative actions might affect the company's profit and solvency, these estimates and analyses help managers plan.

Managers use accounting information to make day-to-day decisions about what activities will best achieve the goals. Management accounting helps managers make these decisions by providing timely economic information about how each activity might affect the organization.

Accounting information also plays a vital role in helping managers control the operations of the company. Managers use the revenue and cost estimates generated during the planning and decision-making process as a benchmark, and then evaluate the company's actual revenues and costs against that benchmark. The deviation between the forecasted and actual numbers has to be explained. Either the forecasting process has to be improved or operational decisions need to be adjusted.

Since managers are making decisions about their own company, the information the management accountant provides is designed to meet the specific information needs of the manager. This involves selecting the appropriate information to be reported, presenting that information in an understandable format, interpreting the information when necessary, and providing the information when it is needed for the decisions being made.

Management accounting varies widely from company to company and the responsibilities and activities continue to evolve in response to the need for new information brought about by the changing business environment. In response to that environment, the Institute of Management Accountants (IMA) publishes guidelines for management accounting called Statements on Management Accounting, or SMAs. The SMAs are nonbinding (they are not rules that must be followed), but management accountants turn to SMAs for help when faced with new situations.

In order to see how a company's accounting information helps managers in their planning, operating, and evaluating activities, briefly consider three key management accounting reports that relate to budgets, cost analyses and manufacturing costs.

1. Budgets

Budgeting is the process of quantifying managers' plans and showing the impact of these plans on the company's operating activities. Managers present this information in a budget (forecast). Once the planned activities have occurred, managers can evaluate the results of the operating activities against the budget to make sure that the actual operations of the various parts of the company achieved the established plans.

For example, a company might report a budget showing how many units of product it plans to sell during the first three months of the year. When actual sales have been made, managers will compare the results of these sales with the budget to determine if their forecasts were "on target" and, if not, to find out why differences occurred. Budgets are powerful planning and control devices.

2. Cost Analysis

Cost analysis is the process of defining the costs of specific products or activities within a company. A manager will use a cost analysis to decide whether to stop or to continue making a specific product. The cost analysis would show that product's contribution to profitability at different levels of sales. Assigning (or defining) costs to products and activities is a complex activity. Every decision-maker in the company has to be familiar with the way relevant costs are assigned in order to make appropriate decisions. Consistency in this reporting process is critical to ensure this information is accurate and has meaning.

3. Manufacturing Cost Reports

As we mentioned above, managers must monitor and evaluate a company's operations to determine if its plans are being achieved. Accounting information can highlight specific "variances" or differences from plans, indicating where corrections to operations can be made if necessary. A manufacturing cost report might show that total actual costs for a given month were greater than total budgeted costs. However, it might also show that some actual costs were greater while others were less than budgeted costs. The more detailed information will be useful for managers as they analyze why these differences occurred.

Internal and External Uses of Accounting Information

Both internal and external users need accounting information to make decisions about a company. Since external users want to see the reported results of management activities, we discuss these activities next. Then we will discuss how accounting information supports management activities and external decision-making.

Presenting Accounting Information

Accounting information prepared for the external user may differ from that prepared for the internal user. Accounting information that helps external users with decisions, such as whether or not to extend a bank loan to a company may be presented differently from the information a manager within the company needs. For instance, if a bank is deciding whether to make a loan, they will consider the likelihood that a company will repay the loan. Since this likelihood may depend on current and future sales of its products, the bank may want to evaluate the sales budget that managers developed as part of the planning process.

Many external users evaluate the accounting information of more than one company, and need comparable information from each company. For example, a bank looks at accounting information from all of its customers who apply for loans, and must use comparable information in order to decide to which customers to make loans. This need for comparability creates a need for guidelines or rules for companies to follow when preparing accounting information for external users. In addition, some external users may have a legitimate need for information generated for internal decision-makers also.

Basic Financial Statements

Companies operate to achieve various goals. They may be interested in providing a healthy work environment for their employees, in reaching a high level of pollution control, or in making contributions to civic and social organizations and activities. However, to meet these goals, a company must first achieve its two primary objectives: earning a satisfactory profit and remaining solvent. If a company fails to meet either of these objectives, it will not be able to achieve its various goals and will not be able to survive in the long run.

Profit, commonly referred to as net income, is the difference between the cash and credit sales of a company and its total costs, or expenses. Solvency is a company's long-term ability to pay its debts as they come due. As you will see, external users analyze the financial statements of a company to determine how well the company is achieving its two primary objectives.

Financial statements are accounting reports used to summarize and communicate financial information about a company. Financial statements are commonly recognized "communication tools" that enable people to assess the financial state of the organization. A company's accounting system produces three major financial statements:

The income statement;

The balance sheet, and;

The cash flow statement.

Each of these statements summarizes specific information that has been identified, measured, recorded, and retained during the accounting process.

Balance Sheet

A company's balance sheet summarizes its financial position on a given date. A balance sheet lists the company's assets, liabilities, and owner's equity on the given date. It is much like a snapshot or where the company's wealth is at a given point in time. The balance sheet is also called a statement of financial position.

Assets are economic resources that a company owns and that it expects will provide future benefits to the company. Anything <u>owned</u> by a company is an asset.

Liabilities are the company's economic obligations (debts) to its creditors-people outside the company such as banks and suppliers-and employees. Anything that is <u>owed</u> by a firm is a liability.

Owner's equity of a company is the owner's current investment in the assets of the company, which includes the owner's original contribution to the company and any earnings (net income) that the owner leaves in the company. A corporation owner's equity is called stockholder's equity.

A balance sheet is arranged into accounts. The value of the asset accounts will always equal the value of the liabilities and owners' equity accounts. This defines the basic accounting equation and is expressed as:

Assets = Liabilities + Owners' Equity

Balance Sheet

Assets		This includes the "stuff" or economic resources that the company has use of and from which it can expect to derive future economic benefit.
Current Assets		Asset that can (will be) converted to cash within the year
	Cash	Cash, currency readily available to the business.
	Accounts receivable	Amount your customers owe because they purchased from you on credit.
	Inventory	The value of the products (merchandise) that has been acquired for sale to customers and is still on hand.
	Total current assets	These are the assets that you use to operate your business- an important part of working capital.
Fixed Assets		Assets that have a long-term use or value-land, building, equipment.
	Property, plant and equipment	The purchase price that you paid for the land, buildings, equipment that you use to create your products or services.
	Accumulated depreciation	How much of the value of your plant and equipment you have used up while operating your business over time.
	Total fixed assets	The net value of your property, plant and equipment.
Total Assets		The value of all of the assets (stuff) of your business.
Liabilities and Owners' Equity		Where the money came from to get the assets. It accounts for who has claims against the assets of the company.
Liabilities		These are "loans" or debt contracts.
Current Liabilities		Loans that have to be paid back within a year.
	Accounts Payable	Amount that you owe your suppliers for materials (inventory) that you purchased on credit.
	Current debt	Loans (part of a long term loan) to be paid back this year.
	Total current liabilities	The debt that you have to pay back within one year.
Long-term liabilities		Loans (or debt contracts) that have to be paid back at some point in the future (more than a year).
Total liabilities		How much of other people's wealth you are renting the use of as if you were using their money on contract.
Owners' Equity		The value of the owners investments in the company.
	Paid-in capital (common stock)	This is the value of what the owners' "paid in" as a direct investment in the company. (corporation - sale of stock)
	Retained earnings	The value of owners' profits that they choose to re-invest in the company.
	Total owners' equity	This is the owners' claim against the assets of the business- or the value of owning the business.
Total Liabilities and Owners' Equity		This will always equal Total Assets- as liabilities and owners equity account for where the money came from to acquire the assets.

The Snap Shot

The balance sheet describes an economic picture of a company at one point in time. This snapshot statement describes the "structure" and current financial condition of the company at a specific point in time. The balance sheet presents a picture of a company and allows you to:

- Compare pictures of two different companies at one point in time and describe the difference, and;
- Compare pictures of the same company at different points in time and describe how it has changed.

Assets are the "stuff" you can use to create transactions. Your best business investment is to put your assets to work and keep them working. Assets include money, buildings, vehicles, equipment and anything the business owns that has value. A related concept to assets is liquidity.

Liquidity

Liquidity relates to the ease with which an asset can be turned into something else. It can turn cash into inventory easily, or what assets are the most liquid. It is hard to turn a building into a fleet of trucks, and therefore, they are considered less liquid.

When the word "current" is used in business, it means "within one year."

Current Assets

Assets that can be converted to cash are called current assets or liquid assets. They include such things as cash, accounts receivable and inventory.

Cash

There are several issues regarding cash management:

- Too little cash on hand can not pay your bills without selling something or taking out more loans.
- Too much cash on hand means that your assets are not working for you as well as they might.

Accounts receivable

You have made sales, but instead of cash, you extend credit. It is like taking an "IOU." The issues involved with allowing someone to pay you after they have received the product or services include:

How long does it take to collect (receivables period)?

How much do you lose for customers who do not pay their bills?

More accounts receivable this year than last indicates either that there is a more liberal credit policy or there are more sales.

The greater the accounts receivable, the less cash there is on hand.

31

About Inventory

> **Raw materials inventory**—When you purchase materials, or component parts, to create the product you make, those are raw materials inventory. If you are a candle factory, purchasing wax and wicks would be an example of raw materials.

> **Work in process inventory**—When you are in the middle of producing or assembling a product at any point in time, committed materials and labor in creating products for sale are referred to as "work in process" inventory.

> **Finished goods inventory**—These are the products you have ready for sale. They are "finished" and ready to be sold to your customers.

The business of the company is to turn cash into inventory and inventory into cash. You acquire materials and transform them. By turning cash into inventory, you create the opportunity to add value into a new product and sell them at a "profit."

Inventory Issues:

- When there is *too much inventory* that you are unable to sell, particularly if these good could become obsolete, significant amounts of cash tied up in products that may not sell for full price. If the products are not desirable, you may have to sell these products at a discounted price or that you have to keep around for a long time. This can be expensive. You may lose money and you may eventually run out of cash.

- When there is *too little inventory* such as in a situation where you are out of stock, customers want your product but are unable to access it. They may forego the purchase or, even worse, buy it from one of your competitors.

Fixed Assets

Fixed assets are things the firm owns that they will use for more than one year. They may include equipment, buildings and vehicles. The value of the company's property, plant (factories, offices, etc.) and equipment is the investment the company has made in itself. It is the "capacity" of the company to create product or services. It is listed at its purchase price. The fact that they are "fixed" assets suggests that they do not have much liquidity—it may take a while, more than one year, to sell these assets and turn them into cash.

Accumulated Depreciation

Fixed assets have a limited life. Trucks need to be replaced, buildings need repair and equipment wears out. Depreciation is the process of recognizing that as you use your building and equipment to create products or services, the value of your fixed assets decrease. These assets are being used up or consumed. Accumulated depreciation is the total amount of value that has been used up since the initial purchase of the equipment.

Total Fixed Assets

Subtracting accumulated depreciation from fixed assets gives you total fixed assets, which is sometimes listed as *property, plant and equipment, net*. Total fixed assets are the current "accounting" value of your property plant and equipment. This number represents the purchase price minus how much of it you have used up over time. This is NOT necessarily the same as the "market value" of your plant and equipment, which is the amount you would receive if you were to sell it. Companies with large accumulated depreciation have aging (old, out-of date or used-up) facilities. These fixed assets are worth much less that those that have been recently acquired.

Total Assets
At one point in time, total assets are the total value of all of the "stuff" you own in your business. It includes both the facilities and the operations at that time. Total assets are a common way to assess how "big" or what "size" a company is.

Liabilities and Owners' Equity
The money to invest in your company's assets and activities has to come from somewhere. In fact, it can come from only two sources; an investment from the owners' investments (owners' equity) or loans (liabilities). Providing money to fund the assets of a company also gives the "providers" a claim against those assets. Owner's claims and debt claims are quite different from one another and companies develop financing strategies to manage these. Financing strategies are plans using debt or owners' investments to operate and grow the company. These strategies consider the differences in the owner's claims and debt claims, the goals of the company, and the nature of the industry in which they are competing.

Liabilities
Liabilities are a form of "debt contracts." You have a contract that allows you to use someone else's wealth in exchange for some "consideration." On most debt, the consideration is an interest payment. This is the "rent" you pay to use someone else's money. A debt contract is for a specific period of time (length of the loan) and you have to return the wealth, or pay back the loan, at the end of the period. Borrowing money increases the amount of cash you have on hand but does not increase your profitability. Paying back your loans decreases the amount of cash on hand but does not decrease your profitability.

Current Liabilities
Current liabilities are contractual obligations (debts) that you have to pay back within the year. Along with current assets, they account for the money it takes for you to operate your business for a given time. Together, current assets and current liabilities are called working capital.

Accounts Payable
Any good supplier wants you to buy from them, not someone else. To make it easier and more attractive to buy, the supplier may offer you the use of their products or materials without payment for a certain number of days. The balance in this account is the amount that you owe to your suppliers for the materials (inventory) that you purchased on credit and have not yet paid for. This is referred to buying on terms and those terms specify the number of days that you have access to these products before having to pay for them. The phrase "net 30" for example, means that you do not have to pay for the product until 30 days after the day you received them. It is attractive for businesses to pay their bills as late as possible, without incurring expensive interest charges, so they can optimize their use of cash.

Current Debt

The balance in this account is the amount of debt. This includes short term loans, which are due in a year, or the current part of a long term loan that needs to be paid back this year.

Total Current Liabilities

Current liabilities are the debts that you have to pay back this year. In general, it is extremely important that you have enough cash (or combination of cash and other current assets) to be able to meet your debt (contractual obligations) for the coming year.

Long-term Liabilities

Loans, or debt contracts, that have to be paid back at some point longer than one year. These could be the not-current part of *long-term bank loans* or *bonds* which are loans that you take directly from the market.

Total Liabilities

This accounts for how much of other people's wealth you are using, or renting using on contract. This number that gives you the total amount of debt the company has and if you divide this number by total assets (or total liabilities and owners' equity), it will tell you what percentage of the assets was funded by debt. This is referred to as the "Debt to Assets Ratio" and can be a valuable measurement tool determining how your total debt compares to your total assets.

Smith's Home Furnishings

This retail furniture store was in the middle of a rapid expansion program. They had opened several stores in a relative short period of time. It appeared that the business was thriving. Rather than paying for these new buildings, however, they were leasing them. They had also made arrangements with furniture manufactures to allow the stores to have the manufacturer's inventory on the show room floor without paying for it. Smith's was a company that owned very few assets and had acquired a tremendous amount of debt. Due to this expansion, Smith's debt to assets ratio was much higher compared to acceptable industry standards and, as a result, the business declared bankruptcy shortly after the Springfield, Oregon store had their grand opening. They did not own enough assets to justify and pay for the debt they had incurred.

Owners' Equity

Owners' equity is a measure of the value of the owners' investments in the company. Generally, accounting systems keep track of how much the owners' pay in (out of their own pockets) and how much of the wealth created in the owners' name, or profits the company creates, is reinvested in the company. The amount that owners reinvest in the company is called retained earnings.

Paid-in Capital (Common Stock)

This is the owners' investment in the company. In a corporation, this is the money received from the sale of common stock. To increase the balance in this account, you have to sell more stock.

Retained Earnings

When a company makes a profit, it belongs to the owners' of the company. Profits can be given to the owners' to use however they want. An owner can decide to do one of two things with profits.

1. They can make a payment out of profits which is called a *dividend.*
2. They can be re-invested back into the company which is called *retained earnings*.

The balance in the retained earnings account is the value of the profits the owners choose to re-invest in the company. The balance in this account and all of the dividends ever paid will equal all of the profits ever made by the company. In both cases, these come from profit the business made.

Total Owners' Equity

This is the owners' claim against the assets of the business or the value of owning the business itself. In a corporation, if you divide this number by the total number of shares, it gives you the value of the claim that each share has against the assets of the company. This is called *book value.*

Total Liabilities and Owners' Equity

This is the value of all of the loans and investments that have been made in the company. Because it describes where the money came from to fund the assets and it describes the claims against the assets of the company, it will ALWAYS EQUAL the value of the total assets of the company.

Two of the accounts are so important that they require additional explanation. The income statement explains the activity in the retained earnings account. This is an owners' equity account that records revenues and expenses. The cash flow statement explains activity in the cash account, or an asset account.

Income Statement

A company's income statement summarizes the results of its operating activities for a specific time period—often one year—and shows the company's profit for that period. It shows a company's revenues, expenses, and net income (or net loss) for that time period. The income statement tracks revenues and expenses.

Revenues are the total of the prices charged to a company's customers for the goods or services the company provides to them.

Expenses are the costs of providing the goods or services.

Net income is the excess of revenues over expenses, or the company's profit; a net loss arises when expenses are greater than revenues.

These amounts include the costs of the products the company has sold (either the cost of making or purchasing these products), the costs of conducting business (called operating expenses), and the costs of income taxes, if any. The result is net income or a loss.

A Simple Income Statement

Income Statement

Revenue		Funds that come into the company from the sale of goods or services. These can be sales that are in cash or on-account.
Variable Costs		A type of cost- those costs that the total costs vary with the level of activity — the more products you make, the greater the total cost.
	Material costs	The cost of the materials (raw material and component parts) that are used in the products you sold.
	Labor costs	The cost of the labor (human resource) used to produce the products sold.
	Inventory carrying costs	The costs (warehousing, insurance, etc) of having inventory available for sale- but not sold.
	Total variable cost Cost of Goods Sold (COGS)	This is the cost of making the products sold.
Contribution Margin		The difference between the revenue brought in by sales and the cost of making the products for sale- this difference is what is left over to operate your business and for profit.
Period Costs		Those costs that are fixed over a period of time. These do not vary with the level of activity.
	Depreciation	This number recognizes the amount of value that operating a business "uses up" the plant (factory) and equipment.
	Research and Development (R& D)	The investment the company makes in developing new products or improving existing ones.
	Marketing expense	The investment the company makes in advertising, selling, and distributing the products.
	Administrative expense	The cost of running a business; legal expenses, accounting services, etc.
	Total period costs	The costs of operating your business over a period of time
Earnings before interest and taxes (EBIT) or Net margin		Revenues minus variable costs (contribution margin) minus period costs.
	Interest expense	The rent you pay to use other people's wealth. This is the expense of your financing strategy.
	Taxes	The tribute you pay to the government as a citizen of a society.
Net Income		Revenues minus variable cost minus period costs minus interest expenses and taxes. This is synonymous with Profit, Earnings, "Return," and "Bottom Line." Creating net income for its owners is the reason for a business to exist.

More on the Income Statement

The income statement is a description of the activity in (transactions that affect) the retained earnings account. These activities are the operating transactions that define the owners' change in wealth. The income statement tells a story about the activity of a company over a period of time. It describes the sales and all of the expenses and defines how much profit was created. Because it is a story of activity, you can use these numbers to measure how well you are doing and you can assess the "goodness" of your decisions in the market.

Revenue

Revenues are the funds coming into the company from the sale of its products or services. It does not matter if the sales are for cash or credit (accounts receivable). Revenues are calculated by:

Revenue = Price (per unit) * units sold

For instance, if you sold 1,000 products at a price of $45 per unit, your revenue is $45,000.

Variable Costs

Variable costs are costs that are directly related to making the *products that you sell*. For instance, if the product you were making was electronic sensors, you would want to know how much each one (each unit) cost to make — $12.00 for the materials and $8.00 for the labor to transform the materials into the finished product. If you add all of the variable costs together, you get a "cost per unit." In this case, the cost per unit is $20. Your total variable costs would be equal to the unit cost multiplied by the number of units sold.

$20 cost per unit * 1,000 units = $20,000 total variable costs

This is the "cost of goods sold." In a period of time, you might make more than you sell and would "spend" more money than is recognized as an income statement expense. An easy way to remember this is that it is the **cost of goods sold**, not the cost of goods produced. If you divide the total variable costs by price, you get a percentage of every sales dollar (revenue) that goes to making the product. The lower this percentage of our cost of goods, the more efficient the company is at making products.

An Introduction to Business

Contribution Margin

The contribution margin is shown on the income statement. The contribution margin number is determined by total revenues minus the variable costs. In the example, it would be:

$$\$45,000 - \$20,000 = \$25,000$$

However, the contribution margin can also be calculated as a per unit number. If the price per unit is $45 and cost per unit is $20, the per unit contribution margin is $25. (If you multiply it the number of units sold, you get the contribution margin on the income statement.)

If you divide the contribution margin by revenue, you get a percentage of each dollar of sale that is left over after you pay for the cost of making the products for sale.

$$20,000/60,000 = 33.33\%$$
$$- \text{ or } -$$
$$\$20 \text{ per unit } / \$60 \text{ per unit } = 33.33\%$$

Therefore, 33.33 cents out of every dollar of sales is left after the cost of producing the products that were sold.

Gross Margin

Gross margin is a related concept to contribution margin, but also recognizes depreciation expenses:

$$\text{Revenue} - (\text{Variable Costs} + \text{Depreciation})$$

By including depreciation, gross margin includes the complete cost of making a product; the cost of material, labor, and the consumption of (or using up) of the equipment. The higher the gross margin, the more efficient the company is in its production. Gross margin is often expressed as a percentage of sales.

$$\text{Gross Profits } / \text{ Net Sales}$$

Period Costs

Period costs include depreciation expenses, research and development expenses and administrative expenses.

Depreciation expense

Depreciation expenses assign an expense to the consumption of the value of facilities and equipment. Depreciation is unique in that it is a **non-cash** expense. It does not cost anything- but it lowers both net income (profit) and taxes. Each year, this expense "accumulates" on the balance sheet.

Research & Development, Marketing and Administrative Expenses

Together, these expenses make up the ongoing of being in business. They are the cost of creating and developing products, marketing and selling them. These also recognize the expenses of making decisions. Managers need to gather information about their environment, about their markets and their customers, and about their operations in order to make effective decisions.

Earnings Before Interest and Taxes (EBIT)

EBIT is a measure of how profitable you are before subtracting the cost of your financing strategy (which is the interest payment).

Interest

Interest payments are the rent you pay on your loans. Generally, the more loans you have, the more risky you are, and the higher interest rate you pay. The interest payment that you have to pay is a function of how much money you owe, how long you are borrowing it, and the rate of interest you are paying. In general, the interest payment is the cost of your financial strategy. The interest, or "rent," you pay on a loan is an expense for having access to money and is an expected part of doing business. Interest is a business expense that reduces your profitability.

Net Income

Net income is the profit a firm creates by engaging in transactions. It is the firm's revenues minus all expenses. The net income generated by a company belongs to the owners of the company. The owners can choose to use this created wealth for personal purposes (take it out of the company) or use the wealth to make the company bigger and more competitive. Because the goal of a business is to make a profit, the net income number is used in a number if measures of business success:

Return on Sales: a measure of how much profit was created for every dollar of sales

$$\text{Net Income / Sales}$$

Return on Assets: a measure of how much profit was created for the assets gathered

$$\text{Net Income / Total Assets}$$

Return on Equity: a measure of how much profit was created with owners' investments

$$\text{Net Income / Owners' Equity}$$

Earnings per Share: a measure of how much profit was created for each share of stock

$$\text{Net Income / Number of shares outstanding}$$

The Cash Flow Statement

A company's cash flow statement summarizes its cash receipts, cash payments, and net change in cash for a specific time period. The cash receipts and cash payments for operating activities, such as products sold or services performed and the costs of producing the products or services, are summarized in the cash flows from operating activities section of the statement. The cash receipts and cash payments for investing activities are summarized in the cash flows. Investing activities include the purchases and sales of assets such as buildings and equipment. The cash receipts and cash payments for financing activities, such as money borrowed from and repaid to banks, are summarized in the cash flows from financing activities section of the statement.

This statement is unique in that it tracks the in-flow and out-flow of cash. For example, when a company spends money to produce inventory, as done in the example below in under "Inventory" for the year 2005 in the far right column, a negative figure in the inventory line represents the value of the cash required for that expense of ($2,353). When that inventory is sold, and evidently that same amount was all sold in the year 2006, that sale generates cash and shows a positive figure of $2,353.

The cash flow statement will also be addressed in the next section with the subject of working capital.

A Simple Cash Flow Statement

	2006	2005
Cash Flows from Operating Activities		
Net Income (Loss)	$2,382	$2,485
Adjustment for non-cash items		
Depreciation	$960	$960
Extraordinary gains/losses/writeoffs	$22	$0
Change in Current Assets and Liabilities		
Accounts Payable	$339	$855
Inventory	$2,353	($2,353)
Accounts Receivable	($902)	$3,647
Net cash from operations	$5,154	$5,593
Cash Flows From Investing Activities		
Plant Improvements	$0	$0
Cash Flows from Financing Activities		
Dividends Paid	$0	($1,000)
Sales of Common Stock	$2,000	$0
Purchase of Common Stock	$0	$0
Cash from long term debt	$0	$0
Retirement of long term debt	($1,000)	$0
Change in current debt (net)	$0	$0
Net cash from financing activities	$1,000	($1,000)
Net Change in Cash Position	$6,154	$4,593
Closing Cash Position	$11,747	$5,593

Note: *Negative cash flows are noted by parenthesis in this example. Negative values may also be noted with a negative sign in front of the number and/or the number shown in red.*

Annual Report

A company may publish its income statement, balance sheet, and cash flow statement along with other financial accounting information in an annual report. A company that is publicly traded, where stockholders have purchased share of the company, is required to publish an annual report to communicate their performance.

For example, you can find Disney's annual report at www.disney.com under the "Investor's Relations" section of their site at :

http://disney.go.com/corporate/investors/financials/annual/2003/index.html

Review and Discussion Questions

1. The accounting system generates information regarding what?

2. Who relies on this information?

3. Cost analysis is best described as what?

4. What are some of the main benefits a well planned budget offers?

5. What are some examples of current and long term assets?

6. Why is it important to know what the contribution margin is on a product basis?

7. What type of information is found on the balance sheet?

8. What type of information is found on the income statement?

9. What is a common problem of inventory management?

10. Describe what depreciation represents.

11. What statement would you refer to in order to find the profit that a company made last year?

12. Where would you find what you invested in advertising last year?

13. Where would you determine what you paid in taxes last year?

14. Look at the Cash Flow Statement example on the previous page. Explain what occurred in the Accounts Receivable in the year 2005 and in 2006.

Chapter 4

Finance: Working and Investment Capital

"Cash is king."
Cash is the single most critical asset in running a successful business.

Key terms to look for:

- Accounts payable
- Bonds
- Book value
- Current ratio
- Debt to asset ratio
- Inventory management
- Leverage
- Line of credit
- Liquidity
- Principal
- Quick or acid ratio
- Stockholder's equity
- Working capital

Finance: Working and Investment Capital

The activities that you engage in to run your business are kept track of in your current assets and current liabilities accounts. Collectively, these are referred to as your working capital. Cash is the most liquid current asset and is critical to running your business.

In its simplest form...

When you operate your company, you turn cash into inventory and inventory into cash through the sales you make. However, to get the cash you need to create inventory, a company might purchase materials on account, referred to as accounts payable, or take a short-term loan from a bank. In order to generate sales, the company might sell on account to make the transaction more attractive. The working capital cycle, also known as the cash flow cycle, is the time between the payments of what a business owes (payables) and the collection of what a business is owed (receivables). Businesses need to manage the amount of time that funds are "tied-up" in order to reduce the amount of working capital needed for operations. This help to make certain that there is adequate cash on hand to operate the business successfully.

Accounting Profit versus Cash Flow

Profits, also referred to as earnings or net income, and cash flow are two different concepts. Profits are defined by accounting rules for an income statement. An accrual accounting system is where the accounting system recognizes transactions when the agreement is made, not when the cash is exchanged. This is opposed to a cash accounting system where it is recognized when the cash is received. Income statements also include non-cash expenses such as depreciation. When using an accrual accounting system, it is possible for a company to be very profitable, and still run out of cash. This may occur when a company is in a growth stage. They are showing a profit, but do not have the cash available to pay their debts. Without cash, the company can go out of business. In addition to managing profitability, the company also has to manage its cash flow: the cash receipts and cash disbursements, or payments over time.

Working Capital Management

Net working capital is the difference between a business' current assets and its current liabilities. Working capital management involves the decisions related to operating the business (working). These decisions will involve the management of cash, accounts receivable, inventories, accounts payable, and short-term bank loans.

Working capital management is concerned with the day-to-day operations rather than long-term business decisions. For example, plans for introducing new products to the market and plans for obtaining the facilities and equipment necessary to produce them are strategic in nature, as are the long-term financing needs of the firm. In general, long-term financing needs are best met through long term sources of capital: retained earnings, sale of stock, and the sale of long-term debt obligations (bonds). Working capital management policies address short-term (issues that occur within the business year) problems and opportunities.

There is a direct relationship between sales growth and current asset levels. For example, higher sales volume may be achieved only if production increases. Higher production, however, requires more money tied up in inventory. Additionally, if a firm buys on credit, its accounts payable increase and when it sells on credit, its accounts receivable increase. Therefore, higher sales require a larger investment in current assets, which requires greater financing. Unless something is really wrong, higher sales mean higher profits. To increase profits, you have to effectively manage your working capital.

The Working Capital Cycle

The working capital cycle includes all the activity between the first cash spent producing a product to receiving a cash payment for its sales. The first step is when the firm orders and receives the raw material, generating an account payable. The last step in the cycle happens when you receive the money owed to you from the sale of the product on credit, which is when the account receivable is paid off.

The working capital cycle is defined as the length of time between the payment of the payables and the collection of receivables. During this cycle, a business' funds are unavailable for other purposes. Cash has been paid for purchases but cash has not been collected from sales. Short-term financing may be needed to sustain business activities for this period. Since there is always a cost to such financing, a goal of any business should be to minimize the cycle. To achieve this goal three terms must be clearly understood:

Production cycle refers to the length of time between purchase of raw material, production of the goods or service, and the sale of the finished product.

Accounts payable lag is the time between the purchase of raw material on credit and cash payments for the resulting accounts payable.

Accounts receivable lag is the time between the sale of the final product on credit and cash receipts for the accounts receivable.

Let's look at examples with different payable and receivables lags. In both examples assume it takes 40 days after an order is received to process the raw material into finished product (production cycle is 40 days).

30 Day AP Lag — In the first example the accounts payable lag is 30 days, and the receivables lag is 45 days. Your company receives the materials and starts to process it. 30 days after receiving the material, you have to pay your supplier (A/P lag), 40 days after receiving the material, you have inventory to sell. For 10 days, your cash is tied up in inventory that is not available for sale. If you deliver it to your customer on the 40th day of the production cycle, your customer has 45 more days to pay for it. On that day, your cash has been tied up in inventory for 55 days (10 days before inventory was ready for sale and 45 days after).

45 Day AP Lag — In the second example the accounts payable lag is 45 days, and the receivables lag is 30 days. Your company receives the materials and starts to process it. 40 days after receiving the material, you have inventory to sell. 45 days after receiving the material, you have to pay your supplier (A/P lag), For 5 days, you have inventory available for sale with none of your own cash tied up. If you deliver it to your customer on the 40th day of the production cycle, your customer has 30 more days to pay for it. On that day, your cash has been tied up in inventory for only 25 days. (You didn't have to pay your supplier for 5 of the 30 days after delivery).

As mentioned before, the working capital cycle represents the time in which working capital is "tied up" in covering production costs. If a business owner is able to shorten the cycle, the need for external financing and the resulting interest expense will be smaller, thus creating higher profits.

Cash and Marketable Securities

You need cash on hand to pay your bills, for example, payment of wages, buy raw materials and pay taxes. The question is: How much cash should you have on hand? You need to be sure you can cover your day-to-day transactions. This amount is called the transaction balance. You might want to keep some extra cash on hand to take advantage of special bargains (a supplier's clearance sale of raw materials), or to take advantage of discounts offered by suppliers for early payment of your bills (accounts payable), or as a precaution against emergencies (any unexpected expense). The cash held for such purposes is called ***speculative cash balances***.

There are many advantages to having sufficient cash on hand and many problems when you do not have enough. However, cash does not work for you. Cash does not earn an explicit return. If you have too much cash on hand, you are not working your assets effectively and your cash is not being used in the most productive manner. As an alternative to holding large cash balances, many companies hold part of their liquid funds in short-term marketable securities. These instruments earn interest and can be very easily converted to cash. Several examples of such securities are:

- ***Treasury Bills*** are short-term loans to the United States government with a smallest denomination of $10,000 and maturing in less than one year. Sold at a discount, the buyer pays an amount less than the face value of the T-Bill but gets the full amount when the bill matures.

- ***Commercial Paper*** is an unsecured loan to a large corporation with good and well-established credit ratings. These loans usually mature between 15 to 45 days (can be from 1 to 270 days).

- ***Certificates of Deposit*** are popular short-term instruments issued by commercial banks. CDs are issued in minimum denominations of $100,000 and may be traded in the secondary market. They are insured by the Federal Deposit Insurance Corporation (FDIC).

Accounts Receivable and Credit Management

The profitability of a business is dependent upon its ability to successfully sell its products for more than it costs to produce them. Offering to sell on credit attracts customers and increases sales volume. There are costs to extending credit that must be understood.

When a company sells product without receiving cash, an account receivable (AR) is generated. You are "loaning" your customer the money to buy your products. Normally, a loan generates some value, usually an interest payment. An account receivable "loan" usually generates value in increased sales, not in a cash interest payment. The total dollar amount of receivables is cash that is "tied up" an unavailable for other uses. This amount is determined by the volume of sales and the average length of time between a sale and receipt of full cash payment:

Accounts Receivable = Credit sales per day x Length of collection period

For example:

> If a business has credit sales of $1,000 per day and allows 20 days for payment, it has a total of $1,000 x 20 or $20,000 invested in receivables at any given time. Any changes in the volume of sales or the length of the collection period will change the receivable position.

A credit policy refers to the decisions to grant, monitor and collect the cash for outstanding accounts receivable. Four factors must be considered in establishing an effective credit policy: credit worthiness standards (can your customers pay you back), credit period (how long do they have to pay), collection policy (what will you do if they do not pay), and discount for early payment (do you give them a discount if they pay early).

Inventory Management

A firm's profitability depends on its ability to sell its products. A company has to have enough inventories to meet demand. How does a company know how much is "enough" inventory? They must forecast and develop sales for a period. Since sales depend on many factors outside of a business' control, inventory management is very challenging. Holding inventory levels at less than what is needed will cost the firm lost sales. On the other hand, holding inventory is expensive and involves costs such as storage and insurance expenses. Holding inventory ties up cash that cannot be used for other purposes. Excess inventory must also be avoided to maximize profits.

Typical questions in determining inventory levels include the following:
- How many units of particular products must the firm hold in stock?
- How many units must be ordered or produced at a given time?
- When should the order be placed?

As mentioned before, in determining how many units to have in stock, sales must be predicted and sufficient inventories held to satisfy the expected demand. Moreover, to prepare for potential sales increases, some level of "safety stocks" must also be held. The amount of safety stock is determined by comparing the cost of maintaining this additional inventory against potential sales losses. The following ratios should help in determine the optimal number of each product in your inventory.

- **Inventory Turnover Rate** = Cost of goods sold / Inventory
- **Inventory Turnover Days** = Number of days in a period / Inventory turnover rate
- **Ideal Inventory** = Cost of goods sold / Industry average turnover rate

For example:

> Last year your business sold goods which cost $100,000 and your average inventory for the year was worth $10,000. The inventory turnover rate for last year was $100,000/$10,000, or 10 times. Furthermore, the business' inventory turnover days were 360 days/10 or 36 days. These numbers indicate that during the past year, your inventory turned over 10 times and, on average, it took 36 days to sell the entire inventory. When compared to industry averages, the relative strength of your business' inventory management will be revealed. A low inventory turnover rate could indicate overstocking, while high inventory turnover days can represent slow sales.

If the average industry turnover rate is 12 times, your business' ideal inventory levels for the year should have been:

$$\$100,000/12 = \$8,333$$

To the extent that both your operations and the industry's operations remain stable, this figure may be used as a guideline for determining inventory levels during the current year.

Total inventory costs include the time value of the capital tied up in inventories, storage and handling expenses, as well as insurance, taxes and cost relating to obsolete inventory. These costs are generally referred to as the inventory carrying costs. Carrying costs always increase as inventory levels rise.

Short-term Liabilities

Short-term credit is any liability with an original payment period of less than one year. Major sources of short-term credit include payables (accounts payable, wages payable, taxes payable) and short-term loans. There are both advantages and disadvantages to using short-term credit.

Speed, flexibility and lower costs are potential advantages of short-term credit. Increased risk to the borrower is considered a disadvantage. Generally, obtaining a longer term loan requires a longer period of time because of the need for a more thorough examination of the borrower's financial statements. Short-term credit, however, usually can be obtained fairly quickly. Also, short-term credit generally requires a lower interest rate which is more cost effective than long-term debt.

Even though short-term debt is often less expensive than long-term debt, short-term borrowers face the possibility of paying higher interest rates as their need for new loans develops over time. Over a couple of years, interest rates may rise significantly. Consequently, short-term borrowing subjects the borrower to uncertain interest expenses as compared with borrowers of long-term funds with locked-in interest rates.

Accounts Payable

Purchasing equipment and raw materials represents a large portion of total operating expenses. A small manufacturing firm may spend in excess of 70 percent of total sales purchasing raw materials and converting them into finished goods (COGS is 70% of sales and Gross margin is

30%). Accounts payable become an important source of financing in the short term. Managing prompt payments of accounts and, keeping repayment cycles as short as is possible make the company an attractive customer.

Short-Term Bank Loans

As a business grows, its needs for "non-spontaneous" sources of credit will grow as well. Commercial banks are major providers of short-term financing to businesses. When applying for a short-term bank loan, select a bank that best serves your needs, and then prepare for a successful loan application interview.

Factors that your banker may evaluate in considering your loan application.
1. *Your character, integrity and overall management skills.*
2. *Your company's track record, i.e. its sales and profits.*
3. *Your product and its relative importance to the market.*
4. *Your financial statements, preferably accompanied by a certified public accountant's statement.*
5. *A description of the purpose of the loan.*
6. *Your company's ability to provide data to the bank both accurately and timely.*
7. *The primary and alternative sources of repayment.*

Factors that your banker may look upon negatively in approving your loan.
1. *Accounts receivable past due, indicating that cash is coming too slowly.*
2. *Accounts payable abnormally extended.*
3. *Poor inventory operation, such as low turnover and large back orders.*
4. *High debt-equity ratio, signifying large outstanding loans.*
5. *Large withdrawals of profits by the company's officers/owners.*
6. *Attempts to borrow short-term funds to meet long-term needs.*
7. *Insufficient financial data.*
8. *Poor credit rating for principal business owners/officers.*
9. *Personal problems of executives.*

The provisions of a loan agreement must be clearly understood by the borrower if they are to know the true costs of the loan. Loan terms can include "hidden" costs or restrictions on business practices.

A *line of credit* is an informal understanding between a bank and a borrower that a specific amount of funds is available for future financing purposes. A *revolving credit account* is a formal line of credit offered to larger businesses in exchange for up-front fees and standard interest payments. In return, the bank has the legal obligation to fulfill its commitments under the formal agreement. Some banks require their borrowers to maintain compensating balances, which usually are a certain percentage of the loan amount. Finally, a lender can require a borrower to pledge collateral as security to ensure repayment of the loan's *principal* and interest.

A Financial Statement Example

Keeping Track: Accounting for all of your transactions

You have an idea — a very good idea — about how to meet the needs of the customers who want electronic sensors. The best part is that you have a competent plan for meeting those needs and making a profit. You put together a business plan, set up a company, and meet with some people (investors) who might want to become part owners of your company. At the end of the meetings, you have convinced 20 investors to give you $1,000,000 each.

When you get home, you decide that you should set up a way to keep track of (or account for) the transactions you will engage in for the company. You want to keep track of both where the money came from and what you are using it for. You know that there are two ways to get money—either from the company's owners (the accounts are called owners' equity accounts) or from some form of a loan agreement (these accounts are called liability accounts). The things you have control over are called assets (and the accounts are called asset accounts). You know that these two systems will always have to account for the same amount of money because the money that you are using has to come from somewhere.

To begin, you set up two accounts: one is for cash which is an asset you have control over, and the other is for the money given to you by the company's owners, called "Paid In Capital" which is an owner's equity account. Because you are dealing with a lot of zeros, you decide to record all of the numbers without the last three zeros and put a note—"all numbers in thousands (,000)." Therefore, your company has control over $20,000,000.

Buying Plant and Equipment
The first step in your plan is to purchase a building (a plant) to manufacture your electronic sensors. The plant and equipment cost $15,000,000. You arrange a loan from the bank for this purchase. The loan agreement requires you to use $5,000,000 of your cash for a down-payment and the bank will let you use $10,000,000 for 10 years. To use the bank's money, you agree to pay them a "rent" of 10% per year (this rent is called interest) and you will return $1,000,000 every year.

This is a complicated agreement to account for. You have the use of a new plant full of equipment that is worth $15,000,000. You set up a new asset account called "Plant and Equipment" and record the purchase price in it. You know that you have $5,000,000 less cash so you subtract that from your cash account. You also know that you owe the bank $10,000,000 and so you start a new account called "Long term Debt" and enter the amount of the loan. You do not "account for" the interest payment or the return of the $1,000,000 until the end of each year so you ignore this information now.

At this point, you have control of a $30M business ($15M cash; $15M plant/equipment). Of that, $20M came from owner's investments and $10M from a bank loan.

Acquiring Inventory

In order to start manufacturing your electronic sensors, you have to purchase the component parts and materials. You locate the parts and materials that you believe will produce the perfect sensor according to your business plan. The businesses you purchase from are called your **suppliers** because they are the source for the materials you need.

The component parts and materials make up your inventory. You agree to give your suppliers $10,000,000 cash in exchange for the inventory you need to begin doing business. You set up a new asset account called "Inventory" and you record the $10,000,000 value in it. You have $10M less cash, so you subtract that amount from your Cash account. The total value of your assets has NOT changed (total = $30M). You have simply changed the form of your assets—what used to be cash, now is inventory.

We are going to begin to build a statement that reflects the impact to our cash flow. This cash flow statement shows assets in the form of cash, our inventory, and our investment in Plant and Equipment. We also see our Liabilities in the form of Long Term Debt and our Owner's Equity which is the Paid in Capital, or "PIC."

Assets				Liabilities	Owners' Equity
Cash	Inv.	Plant/Equip.		LT Debt	PIC
$20,000					$20,000
(5,000)		15,000		10,000	
(10,000)	10,000				
$5,000	$10,000	$15,000		$10,000	$20,000

Based on this, you are so encouraged and optimistic about introducing your new electronic sensor to the market that you revise your plan. You are willing to bet that you will be able to sell even more than you originally forecast. However, it will take $2,000,000 more in inventory. You know that you will need at least $5M in cash to generate sales (for advertising and to develop your sales force) and you do NOT want to spend the cash. You contact your suppliers and discuss your dilemma with them.

51

Your suppliers look at your plan and at your financial records and agree that you should have no problem meeting your revised forecast. They agree to sell you additional component parts and materials but you do not have to pay them for three months. Essentially, they are loaning you the value of the inventory for 90 days. Since loans are recorded in liability accounts, you set up a new one called "Accounts Payable" and record the value of the loan from your suppliers there. You also have an additional $2M in inventory, so you add that value into your inventory asset account. You are still in "balance," but the value of the company you control is now $32M.

We have added some columns to our table. We will expect that we will have current assets and liabilities in the form of accounts receivable and short term debt, respectively. We also see that we are expecting to account for earnings in the "Owner's Equity" area of our cash flow statement.

Assets				Liabilities			Owners' Equity	
Cash	Acct. Rec.	Inv.	Plant/Equip.	Acct. Pay	ST Debt	LT Debt	PIC	Earnings
$20,000							$20,000	
(5,000)			15,000			10,000		
(10,000)		10,000						
		2,000		2,000				
$5,000		$12,000	$15,000	$2,000		$10,000	$20,000	

Improving Equipment

You learn that there is a new kind of computer—it is some type of a robotic device that has been designed to work with the equipment that you have in your plant. You study this problem carefully weighing the benefits of having the automation versus the cost of the equipment. You decide to automate about 25% of your machines at a cost of $3,000,000. You take out a loan for this investment and agree to pay back the whole $3M in the next year (and pay 10% interest on this amount). Because you have to pay back this loan so quickly (within a year), you do not want to add the amount to the loan for the original plant and equipment. You set up a new liability account called "short term debt."

You record the $3M that you will have to pay back in the new account and you add $3M to the value of your Plant and Equipment. The value of the company has increased by this amount to $35M.

Now that you have set up this new account, you realize it would be more accurate to recognize the value of all of the debt that you have to pay within the coming year. That would include $1,000,000 of the original $10,000,000 loan to buy the plant and equipment. You account for this by reducing the Long Term Debt account and increasing the Short Term Debt account by that amount.

Assets				Liabilities			Owners' Equity	
Cash	Acct. Rec.	Inv.	Plant/Equip.	Acct. Pay	ST Debt	LT Debt	PIC	Earnings
$20,000							$20,000	
(5,000)			15,000			10,000		
(10,000)		10,000						
		2,000		2,000				
			3,000		3,000			
					1,000	(1,000)		
$5,000		$12,000	$18,000	$2,000	$4,000	$9,000	$20,000	

For convenience, as you begin accounting for business operations (revenues and expenses), only the account balances (above) will be carried over in the next worksheets.

Operating your business

Now that you are properly set up, you are ready to sell your product. In the first year you sell 1,500,000 units at a price of $10.00 cash. This gives you an additional $15,000,000 cash. When the company makes (or loses) money, this money belongs to the owners of the company. You need to set up a new account - a new owners' equity account- for the earnings of the company. This account is called the "Retained Earnings" account. To account for the cash sales, the value of the cash account and the value of the earnings account both increase by $15M.

The company also sold an additional 500,000 units for $10.00 each, but these were sold on "account." This means that you are owed the money but you do not yet have the cash. You have done this same thing where you had purchased some inventory on account (without having to pay the cash for 90 days) and you made the sale but, have not yet collected the cash. In order to keep track of this kind of transaction, you create a new asset account called "Accounts Receivable," or A/R, in which you record sales we have made but not yet received the money for. The value of sales on account is $5,000,000 (500,000units * $10). The value created by this transaction belongs to the owners and so is recorded in the retained earnings account.

You sold 2,000,000 units from inventory. Each unit has $5.00 worth of materials in it. (This is called the materials cost). To create sales of 2,000,000 units, your reduced the value of your inventory by $10,000,000 (2 million units times $5.00 per unit). This is expense is an owner's expense and is accounted for as a reduction in "Earnings."

Each of the 2 million units sold also had a labor expense. For every unit produced, the company had to pay wages (out of cash) of $2.00. To create sales of 2,000,000 units, it cost the company $4M out of cash for labor. This is expense is an owner's expense and is accounted for as a reduction in "Earnings."

Assets				Liabilities			Owners' Equity	
Cash	Acct. Rec.	Inv.	Plant/Equip.	Acct. Pay	ST Debt	LT Debt	PIC	Earnings
$5,000		$12,000	$18,000	$2,000	$4,000	$9,000	$20,000	
15,000								15,000
	5,000							5,000
		(10,000)						(10,000)
(4,000)								(4,000)
$16,000	$5,000	$2,000	$18,000	$2,000	$4,000	$9,000	$20,000	$6,000

Unit Costs

You are selling electronic sensors for $10.00 each. To make a sensor costs you $5.00 for the materials and $2.00 for the labor to assemble it. If these are all of your costs, each sensor would contribute $3.00 ($10.00 price per unit minus $7.00 cost per unit) toward your profitability. This is called your per unit contribution margin, or margin or per unit contribution to profit.

Material costs and labor costs are variable costs because the total cost varies depending on how many you sell. For instance, if you sell 1,000,000 sensors, your total material cost will be $5,000,000 and your total labor cost will be $2,000,000. If you sell 1,500,000 sensors, your total material cost will be $7,500,000 and your total labor cost will be $3,000,000. Because the total cost varies with the number of units sold, these costs are considered variable.

Period Costs

Your business has other costs that do not vary with the level of sales. While variable costs are measured according to how much business is done (costs that vary by level of sales), period costs measure costs over a specific period of time.

For Example:

>A period cost in your non-business life would be your apartment rent. If you rent an apartment, the cost of rent does not go up or down depending on how many nights you spend in the apartment. The amount of rent is fixed for this period of time, in this case, one month. You must pay the full month's rent regardless of how many night you have stayed in your apartment.

Over the course of the first year, you spend $800,000 on research and development to improve your electronic sensor. You do this because you will have to change your product over time to remain attractive to your customers. This $800,000 comes out of cash and also reduces the owners' earnings. This keeps the balance statement balanced!

In a similar way, you spend $1,200,000 on advertising and $1,000,000 on developing your relationships with your customers. This supports your sales budget and the way that you get product to your customers, through the channels of distribution as you support the efforts of your sales force. These expenses are paid out of cash and reduce the owners' earnings.

Assets				Liabilities			Owners' Equity	
Cash	Acct. Rec.	Inv.	Plant/Equip.	Acct. Pay	ST Debt	LT Debt	PIC	Earnings
$5,000		$12,000	$18,000	$2,000	$4,000	$9,000	$20,000	
15,000								15,000
	5,000							5,000
		(10,000)						(10,000)
(4,000)								(4,000)
(800)								(800)
(1,200)								(1,200)
(1,000)								(1,000)
$13,000	$5,000	$2,000	$18,000	$2,000	$4,000	$9,000	$20,000	$3,000

For convenience, as you continue accounting for business operations (revenues and expenses), only the account balances (above) will be carried over in the next worksheets.

Your goal is to accurately account for the value of the wealth that you are using and creating. A difficult problem is accounting for using up (or consuming) the value of your equipment.

Consider the example of a truck:

> You purchase a new truck for $25,000. You expect it to last for 5 years and have no value at the end of the 5 years, called residual value. When you purchase the truck, your "Plant and Equipment" account shows this $25,000 value. The problem is that at the end of the first year, the truck is not worth $25,000, it in fact, worth something less. Since it has a projected life of 5 years, you have consumed one fifth (1/5 of $25,000 = $5,000) of the total value. To account for this consumption of value, we create a new asset account called Accumulated Depreciation.
>
> At the end of the first year, the truck's $25,000 value is reduced by $5,000. At the end of the 2nd year, the reduction is $10,000; the 3rd year is $15,000; the 4th year is $20,000; and the 5th year is $25,000 reduction.

There are a variety of ways to depreciate your capital equipment. The simplest is straight line depreciation. You start with the purchase price ($18M) and subtract how much it will be worth at the end of its useful life, or its residual value. The difference is "consumed" equally over each year of the plant and equipment's useful life. You expect to be able to use your current plant and equipment for 10 years. At the end of 10 years, it will have a residual value of $8,000,000.

$18M (purchase) - $8M (residual value) = $10M
$10M of value consumed over 10 years is $1M per year

The depreciation expense does not reduce the amount of cash on hand (it is a non-cash expense) but it does reduce the value of the assets you have control over. It also reduces the value of the owners' wealth in the company and so reduces the Earnings.

Assets					Liabilities			Owners' Equity	
Cash	Acct. Rec.	Inv.	Plant/ Equip.	Ac. Depr.	Acct. Pay	ST Debt	LT Debt	PIC	Earnings
$13,000	$5,000	$2,000	$18,000		$2,000	$4,000	$9,000	$20,000	$3,000
				(1,000)					(1,000)
$13,000	$5,000	$2,000	$18,000	($1,000)	$2,000	$4,000	$9,000	$20,000	$2,000

Paying Loan Principal and Interest

At the end of the year, you have to pay the "rent" for using other people's money (interest on the loan) and give back some of the money you are using. These amounts were specified in the original loan agreements or contracts.

Over the past year, you incurred an interest expense on $13,000,000 worth of loans. You agreed to pay the owners' of that money 10% the total value to be able to use it, 10% of $13,000,000 is $1,300,000. This comes out of cash and is an expense that reduces the value of the owners' earnings. This is just one of the costs of being in business.

At the end of the year, you have $4,000,000 in loans that have to be paid back. According to the loan agreements you signed (contracts), you do not have the right to use this money any more. This $4M comes out of cash and reduces the amount of debt that your company has. This return of money reduces the total value of the company; that is, it reduces the amount of wealth that you control and can use to do business. However, it is NOT an expense and therefore does NOT REDUCE the owners' wealth.

Assets					Liabilities			Owners' Equity	
Cash	Acct. Rec.	Inv.	Plant/Equip.	Ac. Depr.	Acct. Pay	ST Debt	LT Debt	PIC	Earnings
$13,000	$5,000	$2,000	$18,000	($1,000)	$2,000	$4,000	$9,000	$20,000	$2,000
(1,300)									(1,300)
(4,000)						(4,000)			
$7,700	$5,000	$2,000	$18,000	($1,000)	$2,000	0	$9,000	$20,000	$700

Financial Statement Conclusion

Each of the account balances change when certain transactions take place. A **Balance Sheet** is a summary of the account balances at a specific point in time. It is a "snap shot" of the company's financial condition and summarizes all of the transactions that have occurred from the start of the company until that point in time.

Two of the accounts, Cash and Retained Earnings, can provide additional useful information if they are summarized separately. Transactions over a specific period of time that affect the Retained Earnings account are summarized in an **Income Statement**. It details the revenues coming into the company and the expenses occurred by the company over that time period.

It is possible to make money (have positive earnings) and still run out of cash. If you run out of cash, you can not continue to do business. The **Statement of Cash Flows** describes the changes in your cash account over a period of time.

Investment Financing: Getting money to grow your business

Companies that are growing always need more money to fuel their growth. They need money to develop new products, to buy new equipment, and to take advantage of opportunities in the market as they emerge.

Individuals or organizations who might provide money that will allow you to grow your business want something from you. It is an economic transaction that follows the rules of all economic transactions. People will only participate if they are made better off through the transaction.

There are basically two kinds of transactions that will get you the money:
1. Taking out a loan (debt contract)
2. Taking on new owners.

Both of these transactions provide cash to help the business thrive. In all other ways they are quite different.

For example:

If I have money to invest, it represents wealth that I have created in the past and not yet consumed. I could use that wealth to buy tools that would allow me to create something of value that I could take to the market. This investment in myself would give me a greater ability to create wealth in the future. However, if I am not going to use it myself, I still want to put it to work. I want that money to work for me as hard as it can, 24 hours a day. I want it to work so I do not have to. One of the things I can do is let others use of my money to create wealth that will come back in some form.

If I am a person who has money to invest, what do I want out of the transaction? I want the highest return I can get for my money and I want to be sure that I do not lose my money. The degree of certainty (or uncertainty) that I will get my money back is the "risk." In a market system, I have a lot of choices about how to put my money to work.

I might be attached to my money and only want it to work in a safe and secure environment where it was sure to be returned to me safe and sound. If that is what I want, I would only "rent" my money to people who were going to use it conservatively. Maybe I would rent it to the government, they can guarantee its safe return. The problem is that everything else being equal (which it isn't) there are a lot of people willing to put their money out to a safe use. When there is a lot of money competing to be put to a safe use, it is easy for those "safe users" (electric utility or government) to get the use of that money cheaply. For the person investing the money, the "return" is expected to be low.

On the other hand, I might be willing to risk my money and give it to someone who will use it in a venture that just might not work out economically. It may represent risk. For instance, I might put my money to work in a biotech firm. They always need more money to create useful mutant biological stuff. The problem is that at this point, a low percentage of the biotech projects work out. However, the ones that do work out economically make huge amounts of money. To rent your money or attract your interest, they have to offer you a high return on your money.

A common rule is:

The higher the risk, the greater the expected return.

Loans

A loan is basically a form of a rental agreement. If I were borrowing money from you, I would be renting the use of your wealth (the amount you borrow is the principal of the loan) At the end of that loan period, I would be expected to return your wealth in good condition. I am renting your money for a specific period of time (term of the loan) and paying you a fee for the use (interest) of that money. Almost always, the fee for using other people's wealth is a percentage of the money you are renting and called the interest rate.

In business, your venture's risk can be a function of the industry you are in, your strategy for competing in that industry, and your experience in serving this market. Your financing strategy, or the way you go about getting the money you need to grow your business, also influences your risk. The more debt you have the more risky you are exposed to. Debt involves a contract whose terms you must meet. If you do not meet your obligation (make your payment), the contract usually specifies a remedy, This may include your creditor being able to force you to sell your assets until you can meet your contractual obligations. When this happens, you are in the process of going out of business. The greater the percentage of assets acquired by debt, the greater the possibility that you would be forced to sell key assets to meet your obligations.

In Foundation™

All companies in Foundation face the same market risks and therefore, the proportion of your assets financed by debt determines your risk level. This risk measured by the debt/assets ratio. When your debt to assets ratio approaches 80%, the banks will not lend you any more money and will charge you the highest interest rate possible. Keeping your dept to assets ratio at an acceptable level—below 80% in this case—will allow you to have access to more affordable capital to operate and expand your business.

An Introduction to Business

Borrowing money increases the total value of your company and infuses cash into the business, but this money is not income. The transaction involves increasing the balance of your cash account and increasing the value of the appropriate liability account. Paying back the loan reduces the balance in your cash account (and the value of your company) and the balance in the appropriate liability account.

IMPORTANT:

Paying down the principal of a loan is not an expense. However, the interest that you pay to use or "rent" the money is a legitimate business expense. Interest expenses reduce the balance in your cash account and the balance in your retained earnings account. Because is comes out of retained earnings, it is a part of (and expensed) on the income statement and reduces your net profits. The more you borrow, the higher the interest rate and the higher the interest payment.

In Foundation™

You can borrow in four ways:
1. Purchase inventory (materials) on credit from your suppliers (short term)
2. Take a short term loan (1 year) from the bank
4. Take a long-term loan from the market (selling a long-term debt called a bond.)
3. Take an emergency loan (a short term loan that is expensive!)

Instead of going out of business and instead of selling off your assets, you may be forced to take an emergency loan. This is an expensive loan that you must pay back within the next year and it drives your interest rates up. You want to avoid an emergency loan whenever possible by using solid financing strategies as you invest in your business.

Accounts Payable

When you purchase materials on account you increase the balance in your inventory account and you increase the balance in your accounts payable account. You are borrowing the use of materials from your suppliers to create products. When you sell the products, you will have the required cash to pay back your suppliers. As mentioned earlier, the amount of time you can use these materials for is called the Accounts Payable lag. As your A/P lag gets larger, your suppliers become more reluctant to provide more materials. If you do not have the materials, you can not produce product and the actual number of units produced in a period is decreased and reflected on the production strategy sheet.

Short-term Loans from a Bank

Banks are financial institutions that accept deposits and make loans. They fall into several categories, such as savings and loans, thrift institutions and commercial banks. Knowing the category in which they include themselves can tell you a lot about the kinds of loans these banks are interested in making. Savings banks are more experienced in dealing with consumer loans, such as home mortgages and automobile loans. Commercial banks have more experience and interest in business loans. The most important point to keep in mind when dealing with a bank is that bankers avoid risk. Their primary concern is always the safety of their funds. A bank will have a company fill out an application, document their financial history (past Balance Sheets and Income Statements), and submit a business plan to assess future potential financial success. In Foundation, your risk is determined by the percentage of assets that are financed by loans, determined by the debt to asset ratio.

A Short-term loan

In the real world, if you run out of money, you have to sell assets to meet your obligations. Once you start selling assets that you could still use productively, you are in the business of going out of business.

Bond (long term financing)

When you borrow money from a bank, you sign a debt contract to use the bank's money for a certain period of time and paying a specific rate of interest. You might have to pledge specific assets as security, or collateral, for the loan. If you should miss payments, the bank can force you to sell the asset and use that money to retire the loan. The terms of this contract are set for the duration of the loan.

Companies and government entities can develop a similar debt contract, but instead of borrowing money from a bank, they can borrow money directly from investors. These debt contracts are called bonds. Bonds are referred to as *securities* because they represent secured (or asset-based) claim for the investors. Stocks are another type of security -secured or asset-based claims against the company- both are traded in *securities markets*.

The debt contract is called an "indenture" and contains the critical information of a loan including answers to these questions:

- Who is borrowing the money?
- How much money is being borrowed?
- For what period of time?
- At what rate of interest?
- How and when is the loan going to be paid off?
- How will the loan amount be secured?

When you borrow money from a bank, you provide information in the loan application that helps the bank determine how likely you are to meet the terms of the contract. The bank uses this assessment to determine whether or not to loan you the money and how high an interest rate they should charge. The higher the risk of non-payment, the higher the interest rate you have to pay. It is impractical for every investor who might want to buy a bond (loan some money) to assess the risk of the company (or government entity) who is issuing the bond. Instead, a few well-established companies, such as Moody's or Standard & Poors, will assess the company and the bond issue and assign it risk rating. The ratings range from AAA, which is excellent, to a bond rating of D, which indicates a high level of risk.

Bond ratings progress from excellent to poor in this order:

Bond Ratings

Excellent	**AAA**	*Low Risk*
	AA	
	A	
	BBB	
	BB	
	B	
	CCC	
	CC	
	C	
	DDD	
	DD	
Very Poor	**D**	*High Risk*

The lower the bond rating, the higher the interest rate the issuing company expects to pay in order to attract investors. Companies get very concerned when their bond rating is degraded. It communicates a negative message to the financial community and to the market in general.

The Bond Market
When bonds are first issued, the company who wants to issue the bond has to get permission from the *Securities and Exchange Commission* (a federal agency). The company then typically goes through an ***investment bank***. An investment bank is a financial institution that specializes in issuing and reselling new securities such as stocks and bonds. The financial managers of the company and the investment bankers go through the reasons for the bond issue (what are they borrowing money for), how long they want to borrow the money, how much money they want, and how much interest they expect to pay.

The investment bank then works to market the new bond issue. They contact big investors — such as banks, insurance companies, pension funds — to determine the willingness of the market to buy and to create a distribution network for the bond issue. They also *underwrite* (buy) a significant portion of the bond issue. This first sale of the newly issued security is in the **primary securities market**.

Because bonds are a secured claim, investors who own them can buy and sell them to other investors. These transactions occur in the *secondary securities markets (or exchanges)* or the "bond market". In the bond market, the bond (debt contract) can trade above or below the face value of the bond. In general, bond prices move in the opposite direction of interest rates — as interest rates fall, bond prices go up and as interest rates rise, bond prices drop.

A bond is an investment whose return is specified in the debt contract. Consider a very simple example; A $1,000 bonds that pays 10% interest per year for 5 years.

As an investor, you see the investment like this:

YEARS	"Bond A"
Year 1	$100
Year 2	$100
Year 3	$100
Year 4	$100
Year 5	$100 + $1,000
TOTAL	**$1,500**

Because this is a contract, this return on your investment does not vary at all. Suppose as an investor, you had the opportunity to choose between buying the 5-year, 10% bond or a new, 5-year, 15% bond (assume equal "risk" or bond rating). If the two investments looked like this, which would you choose?

YEARS	"Bond A"	"Bond B"
Year 1	$100	$150
Year 2	$100	$150
Year 3	$100	$150
Year 4	$100	$150
Year 5	$100 + $1,000	$150 + $1,000
TOTAL	**$1,500**	**$1,750**

The rational investor would pick the investment with the higher return – "Bond B" paying 15% interest. However, if the investor who owned "Bond "A" was motivated, she might offer to sell it at $980. If she attracted no buyers, she might offer it at $960, then $940, and then … at some lower price, the potential buyer would be as well off buying "Bond A" as "Bond B". As the return on the alternative investment (interest rate of the other bond) goes up, then the trading price of existing bonds goes down.

Consider the same scenario, but the alternative bond offers a 5-year, 5% return.

YEARS	"Bond A"		"Bond C"
Year 1	$100		$50
Year 2	$100		$50
Year 3	$100		$50
Year 4	$100		$50
Year 5	$100 + $1,000		$50 + $1,000
TOTAL	**$1,500**		**$1,250**

The rational investor would want to buy bond "A". So would other investors. The current owner of "Bond A" faces a situation where there are motivated buyers competing to buy his investment. They would bid the price of a 10% bond higher than the face value ($1,000) because the return is better than any alternatives. At some price, say $1,120 for discussion purposes, the two investments would be equally attractive and would generate buyers. A $1,120 price for a bond that pays $1,500 would be about as attractive as a $1,000 price for a bond that pays $1,250.

Bonds are bought and sold every day on the bond market. At the end of a trading day, the information about the outstanding bonds, the value of their issue, their trading prices, yield, and the bond rating of the company are published in the financial press

Company	Issue	Value	Yield	Close	S&P
Digby	10.8S2013	$4,347,878	10.3%	105.16	AA
	13.2S2014	$23,000,000	11.4%	115.48	AA

In this instance, the company "Digby" has two different issues of bonds outstanding.

The first bond "10.8S2013" is:
An issue that pays 10.8% and each year until the bonds matures in 2013.
One that when they issued this series, they received $4,347,878.
Currently trading at 105.16% of its face value.
Showing a face value of the bond was $1,000, it would currently cost you $1,051.60 to purchase one of these bonds.
One with a 10.8% return on a price of $1,051.60 is a real return, or yield, of 10.3%.

The second bond "13.2S2014" is:
An issue that pays 13.2% each year until the bond matures in 2014.
A significant issue raising $23,000,000.
Currently trading at $1,154.80 for a $1,000 face value bond.
Showing a purchase price of $1,154.80 on a 13.2% bond provides a real yield of 11.4%.

The company has a AA bond rating based on its current financial status.

In Foundation™

When you sell new bond issues, the interest rate you have to pay is 1.4% higher than your short-term rate. You would choose to do this if you thought you might have to borrow more money in the future. The more you borrow, the higher your risk, the higher the interest payment you have to pay. It does not take very long before your short term rate will be above the 1.4% premium making the earlier decision to "lock in" an interest rate for the term of the bond a better decision. When you issue new bonds, there is a commission that you have to pay to the investment bankers to help you issue the new bonds. The year your bonds mature, they are transferred from long-term debt to short-term debt and automatically paid off. The amount you pay is the amount of the bond issue (column 3). Your bond price goes up and down depending on the interest rate. If you want to retire bonds, or buy back your bonds before they come to maturity, you have to pay the closing price.

Stockowner's Equity

When you sell shares of stock, you are selling ownership rights to a corporation. Owners, or stockholders, never have to be paid back, and you do not have to pay them interest on the money that they are investing in the company. However, owners have a claim against the assets and the wealth that is created in the form of net income, earnings, and profit by the company. That ownership claim *never* ends. This ownership lasts as long as the organization does and the owners will continue to have a say in the management of the company.

Stock Market

When you own a stock, you are actually a part of the owner of a corporation. As a shareholder, you have a "say" in how the company operates, although you voice may be one of thousands of other shareholders.

Companies initially issue stock to raise capital to run their business — often motivated by the fact that they need more money. A corporation sells shares to investors in an organized fashion called a public offering, the fist of which is its initial public offering, or **IPO**. After the company's IPO, investors are free to sell their shares and buy more, but not from the company directly. Instead, share are traded on organized stock markets like the New York Stock Exchange and NASDAQ.

A company can issue common stock or preferred stock. **Common stock** represents a simple share of ownership and each common stock share has one vote to cast when electing the corporation's Board of Directors. If the company were to go bankrupt, the corporation would have no financial liability to common shareholders, and those shares may become worthless.

Preferred stock, a form of stock that traded at a far lower volume than common stock, does have the privileges. Preferred shareholders, often having some kind of history or relationship within the company, may receive higher dividends and have a first claim to assets if a company should go bankrupt, for example.

Shares of stock are traditionally represented by a piece of paper, or a stock certificate. As shares of stock trade electronically, you may never actually see a physical certificate for the share that you own. The brokerage holds the shares on your behalf in what is know as a "street name," which is nothing more than a method of bookkeeping and how no affect on your ownership of the stock. Owning shares in street name is much more efficient and convenient, especially when it is time to sell the stock.

Like a bond, stocks are secured investments. They have a claim against the assets of the company. The company sells new shares of stock to potential owners through the *primary securities market* in a process similar to the way new bond issues are sold. The company meets with an investment banker who reviews the business strategy and specific plans for the money that is to be raised. The investment bank underwrites or buys, markets and distributes the new shares. Underwriters charge a commission and also makes money by holding some of the shares until the price per share raises. Again, once stock has been issued, owners can buy from and sell to others on the ***secondary securities markets*** *(exchanges)* in "stock markets" in the US and numerous exchanges throughout the world. The company itself receives no cash for shares that are sold in the secondary markets and every corporation wants to see its stock price increase for the benefit of the shareholders and the financial reputation of the corporation.

If you are a potential investor in a company (someone who is thinking about purchasing shares of stock in a company), you have choices about which company you would purchase shares in. You want to invest your money is a company that is going to work your money and create as much wealth for you as is possible.

There are two ways in which your wealth increases by owning stock:
   1. When the value of your shares increases as the stock price goes up; and,
   2. When the company distributes the profits it has created in the form of a cash payment to owners out of net income called dividends.

Paying Dividends
When a company creates profit, the profit belongs to the owners. There are only two things that can happen with that profit:
   1. It can be kept in the company as retained earnings; or,
   2. It can be distributed to the owners in the form of a cash disbursement or payment. If it is paid out to the owners, it reduces the amount of cash on hand.

For example:

> As an owner, I might wish to invest in a company that pays a regular dividend. For instance, if I were retired I might want to have 10,000 shares of stock in a company that regularly pays $4 per share dividend. I would know that every year, I would receive $40,000 in cash for me to live on. I would think this dividend policy added to the value of the shares of stock I purchased and would consider this in deciding how much I might be willing to pay for that stock.

In Foundation™

Dividends should be paid from the profits of the business. It is generally not a good idea to pay dividends in a year when you are borrowing money. Owners and the market for potential owners interpret this as borrowing money to pay the dividend. The owners gave the managers of the company their money to grow their wealth, not for the managers to take out loans in their name. Owners do not like managers to hold "excessive" cash balances. It is their money and they expect it to be working hard to create more wealth. Cash does not earn any return. They think that if you do not have a productive use for their cash, you should give it back to them by paying a dividend. A productive use is to invest in new products, make facility improvements, and act on other decisions that will put that cash to work for the business.

Ratios, Value and Stock Claims

The interaction of buyers and sellers of the stock determine stock price. A potential buyer might consider three things in determining how much they would be willing to pay to own stock in a particular company:

- The value of the stock's claim against the assets of the company.

- How much profit the company makes per share of stock.

- How much of that profit do they distribute to owners (in form of a dividend).

The value of this claim is determined by dividing the total owners' equity from the balance sheet by the number of shares outstanding. For instance, if the value of the owners' claim is $100 million and there are 2 million shares of stock issued and outstanding, then each share has a claim against the assets of the company worth $50. This is called the **book value** of the stock.

There are two ways to increase book value; increase the value of total owners' equity or reduce the number of shares outstanding (buy back stock). The easiest way to increase owners' equity is to make a profit and reinvest it, or retain it, in the company which increases the value of the "retained earnings" account. If you sell more shares to increase the value of the "common stock" account, you have increased the value of total owners' equity, but you have also increased the number of shares you have to divide it by in order to get book value.

In general, current owners would prefer that you borrow money to grow the company, if you can afford the interest payments, rather than dilute the value of their claim.

Leverage is a concept that measures how big of a company the managers have created using the owners' investment. Leverage is measured by:

Leverage = Total Assets / Total Owner's Equity

Assume that owners have invested a total of $1 million.

In the first example, the managers have created a company whose total assets are $1.5 million. The leverage ratio is:

$1.5 million / $1 million = $1.5 million

How could the managers create a $1.5 million company with an owners' investment of $1 million? Remember, the accounting equation is;

Assets = Liabilities + Owners' Equity

They can accomplish this by borrowing the $.5 million. The managers have created a company 1.5 times as big as the owners' investments by borrowing additional capital.

In the second example, the managers have created a company whose total assets are $5 million. The leverage ratio is;

$5 million / $1 million = $5 million

Managers in this company used the initial $1 million investment to borrow an additional $4 million. They created a company five times as big as the owners' investments.

In general, as an owner with a $1 million investment, one would rather own a $5 million company than a $1.5 million company. I want my managers to borrow money, as long as it makes economic sense, rather than to sell stock.

Measuring Profit Per Share

The goal of a business is to make a profit. Interest payments on loans reduce profits. As an owner, I am interested in how much new wealth (profit) the company makes per share of stock. I want them to make as much as possible. Earning per share (EPS) is a ratio that calculates profit per share:

EPS = Net Income / Number of shares

If a company with one million shares of stock outstanding creates a net income of $10 million, the EPS would be $10 per share. Clearly, the way to maximize this number is to make as much profit as possible while keeping the number of shares as low as possible. In addition, remember that owners have a claim against all future profits of the company. The company made $10 per share this year, an owner might anticipate earnings at least that good in the future. This anticipation of future earnings also influences how the value of a share is determined.

Large volumes of stock are commonly traded every day. At the end of the day, the transactions in the market are summarized so investors can study what has been happening and make informed decisions about future purchases.

Company	Close	Change	Shares	Dividend	Yield	P/E	EPS
Andrews	$51.29	$22.48	2,000,000	$2.00	3.9%	5.8	$8.88
Baldwin	$69.86	$21.09	2,157,790	$0.50	0.7%	5.6	$12.49
Chester	$41.26	$6.75	2,045,860	$1.00	2.4%	6.8	$6.04
Digby	$37.40	$10.60	4,096,380	$2.00	5.3%	8.1	$4.61
Erie	$15.82	($0.47)	3,209,871	$0.00	0.0%	18.0	$0.88
Ferris	$65.20	$24.76	2,339,022	$3.00	4.6%	6.0	$10.84

In the above table, the trading of six company's stocks is summarized. Let's use Andrews as an example.

- At the end of the trading day, Andrews stock was selling at (valued by buyers) $51.29 per share.

- Because this is $22.48 higher than the close at the end of the last trading period, the last closing price was $28.81 (28.81 + 22.48 = $51.29).

- Andrews has 2 million shares of stock outstanding. Last year, they paid a dividend of $2.00 to each of those 2 million shareholders (which would reduce their cash by $4 million ($2 * 2 million).

- This $2.00 payment represents a 3.9% return (yield) on the $51.29 stock price (2 / 51.29 = .03899 = ~3.9%).

Therefore, each share of Andrews' outstanding stock (2 million) has earned $8.88 of net income (Earnings Per Share). Their total net income must have been $17.76 million (2 million times 8.88).

The ratio in the next to the last column is the Price/Earnings ratio , or the PE, which measures how many times you would have to multiply the earnings to get the stock price. Andrews' stock is trading at 5.8 times as much as they earned in this one year.

Other Important Ratios

Investments in current assets represent a substantial portion of a small business' total assets: up to 70 percent of total business spending may be used for purchases of supplies, and raw materials. Additionally, about 40 percent of a typical firm's capital is represented by its current assets value. Therefore, proper management and use of current assets and current liabilities is crucial to the health and survival of any small business.

Three ratios allow a comparison of your business with your competitors and to industry averages. These ratios also play an important role in the granting or denial of loan requests. Managers should calculate and monitor these financial ratios as part of their working capital management policy.

Current Ratio   =   Current assets / Current liabilities

Quick or Acid Ratio   =   (Current assets - Inventories) / Current liabilities

Debt to Total Assets Ratio   =   Total debt / Total assets

The current and quick ratios measure liquidity and reveal whether the firm can meet its debts for the coming year. The debt-to-asset ratio shows the degree of financial leverage.

Using the Cash Flow Statement as a Management Tool

It is important that managers ensure that the business always has enough cash on had to purchase and pay for the materials and human resources it need to produce gods and services. The Cash Flow Statement can be a valuable tool to determine how much cash is available now and how much will be available in the future and when. This activity, called cash flow management, requires careful planning. Although sales may be booming, if sufficient cash is not available to pay the expenses for the month, the firm will not have funds to pay for them. This may result in a costly "emergency loan" or potentially in bankruptcy. If excess cash balances are allowed to sit idle instead of being invested, a firm loses the potential opportunity for cash returns that it may have earned.

Review and Discussion Questions

1. What is a dividend?

2. What does earnings per share measure?

3. How is capital acquired through the finance department?

4. If you sell products on credit, how is that transaction recorded?

5. What does return on sales (ROS) measure and what relevance might that provide?

6. What insight might return on equity (ROE) provide?

7. What does leverage measure? What might a radical change in leverage from year to year indicate?

8. Discuss the potential relationship between gross sales and profits.

9. What does stock represent?

10. What might be the ramifications, financially and from a marketing perspective, of increasing the account receivable lag time?

Chapter 5

Production:
Improving productivity and performance

*Efficiently managing resources, such as people and equipment,
to produce and provide quality products and services.*

Key terms to look for:

- Benchmarking
- Capacity
- Carrying costs
- Economies of scale
- Human resources
- Materials requirement planning (MRS)
- PERT chart
- Quality control
- Raw materials
- Supply chain management (SCM)
- Total quality management (TQM)
- Work-in-process inventories

Production: Improving productivity and performance

Production is the process by which a company produces finished goods and services. This process might involve the work, ideas, and plans of the design engineers, the production manager, the plant manger, the plant superintendent, their crews and any other department actually involved with producing the product. Production can take the form of mass production, when a large number of standard products are created in a traditional assembly line process, or refer to more specialized production when individual or small quantities are created.

A business needs a production process whenever it provides products or services. This involves a series of tasks where resources are used to create a product or service. This process involves planning, procuring goods to produce the products, assigning tasks and organizing tasks to make those products available for sale. It is important to differentiate production from operations. **Operations** are the functions needed to keep the company producing through a function or series of functions to carry out a plan while **production** involves the actual process to create goods and services.

Production management seeks to develop an efficient, relatively low-cost and high quality production process of creating specific products and services. Production management can contribute to the success of both manufacturing firms and service-oriented firms. The profits and value of each firm are influenced by its production management process.

The primary resources that firms use for the production process include:
- Human resources — *employees and their skills involved in the production process*
- Raw materials — *cost of goods to create the products*
- Capacity — *production facilities, technology, machinery and equipment*

These resources cost money. Employees need to be paid, materials have to be purchased, and building and production facilities take time and money to be ready for production. The objective is to use these resources in the most efficient manner possible. This will enable the organization to take advantage of higher production levels producing more units at a lower cost per unit.

Economies of scale may be one of the objectives. **Economies of scale** describe the process where the cost of each good produced decreases with higher volumes. Variable costs — those associated with the number of goods produced— and fixed costs—costs that do not change regardless of volume—are monitored throughout this process. As output increased, fixed costs remain the same and variable cost on a per unit basis typically decline as production volumes increase.

Scheduling

The production manger or team is responsible for producing goods or delivering services. This role is concerned with volume, production sequence, and the type of product to be produced. Three elements of management — planning, organizing and controlling — can clearly be seen in the tasks of the production manger.

A *master production schedule* determines when the products will be produced and in what quantities. Dates must be met, specified quantities must be produced on time, and costs need to be controlled to make certain this process goes smoothly and meets commitments. One tool to help with this process is a *PERT chart*. Pert stands for program evaluation and review technique. This is a graphical representation to track the events with their respective time frames from start to finish. It describes the process, maps out the time required, and can identify problems in the process before it begins.

Inventory Control

As goods are produced, they also need to be managed. Inventory control is the process of efficiently managing inventory. There need to be enough products available for sale, but there should not be too much product unnecessarily tying up cash. An efficient inventory control system controls the costs associated with inventory.

Companies must also manage their products as they are being created. This is described as *work-in-process inventory*, or products that are only partially completed but have required an investment of some type of resource. Products cannot be sold until they are complete and monitoring the status of these products still involved in production is important.

Another cost directly associated with inventory is carrying costs. *Carrying costs* are the costs of maintaining inventories. A popular method for reducing carrying costs is the just-in-time (JIT) inventory system. This system is based upon having just enough inventory on hand to satisfy consumer demand. Product should always be available, but there is not and overstock of what is needed for the near future. JIT may be in conflict with economies of scale goals and the organization need to balance these decisions.

The just-in-time system is often associated with a materials requirement planning process that ensures that materials are available when needed. A *materials requirement planning* system or MRP helps to determine when the materials to produce the product are needed to meet production deadlines. As a firm develops a forecast for the demand for its products, it determines the time at which the materials need to arrive at the production site to meet the anticipated market demand.

The collection of partners — manufacturer, wholesaler, distributor, retailer, online sales site — is referred to as the supply chain. There has been an effort to improve the relationship with manufacturers and their suppliers. This effort is referred to as *supply chain management (SCM)* and the objective is to manage the connection between supply chain members to enhance efficiencies and reduce costs.

Supply chain management involves these five basic components:

- Plan – *the strategic plan to manage all of the resources that go into meeting customer demand for your product or service*
- Source – *The selection of the supplies that will deliver goods and services*
- Make – *The manufacturing step involving scheduling, testing, packaging and preparing for delivery.*
- Deliver – *The logistics and timing of getting those product and/or services through the channel.*
- Return - *The "soft" link in the chain that supports customers returning product or have had problems with the experience.*

Companies such as Hewlett-Packard and Xerox, among others, have developed systems that have produced dramatic results. Cisco Systems and others have developed software and web-based programs to assist organizations as they work to realize greater efficiencies in their supply chain process.

In Foundation™

Companies are charged an inventory carrying cost of 12% of the average cost of production for unsold units remaining at year end. Keeping inventory levels at an acceptable range — more than one unit and less than 60 days inventory based on what was actually sold that year— will be advantageous to keep these carrying costs to a minimum. This presents a tremendous challenge. Your production volumes will be driven by your sales forecast and therefore, relate to your anticipated market share. All of these variables for each product will determine your production and resulting inventory levels.

Quality Control & Total Quality Management

Quality is the degree to which a product or service satisfies a customer's expectations. Quality relates to consumer satisfaction and is a factor regarding the firm's current and future success. Quality control is the process of testing to determine if the product or service meets the performance and other set standards of the organization before it is sold. Techniques to monitor quality may include sampling, monitoring customer/user complaints and looking to correct deficiencies.

In some cases, quality standards are set by agencies, such as the Food and Drug Administration (FDA) and the Consumer Products Safety Council (CPSC) or by industry associations. The standards imposed by these entities affect the design, performance, durability, safety and many other attributes of how the goods will perform and function. Quality is also used as a competitive advantage to provide "perceived excellence" compared to other consumer choices on the market.

Several techniques are used to improve quality within an organization. ***Quality circles*** are small groups of employees who meet regularly to identify and attempt to solve problems to improve quality. A more formalized process is the concept of ***Total Quality Management (TQM)***.

Total Quality Management is the act of monitoring and improving the quality of products and services produced. This concept is based on the work of W. Edwards Deming and, among others, includes these guidelines:

- To provide managers and other employees with the education and training they need to excel in their jobs.
- To encourage employees to take responsibility and to provide leadership.
- To encourage all employees to search for ways to improve the production process.

Many firms create teams of employees to assess quality and offer suggestions for continuous improvement. This creates a form of cross functional teamwork where employees with different jobs, responsibilities and perspectives work together toward improving the production process through enhanced quality.

The process called benchmarking is another quality improvement technique. The term ***benchmarking*** describes a method of evaluating performance by comparison to another specified level achieved by another entity. For example, Ford Motor Company studied and used the customer service performance levels of Eddie Bauer to improve their customer relations process. Benchmarking may be used in conjunction with a TQM process.

In Foundation™

An optional Total Quality Management (TQM) initiative integrated into the Foundation experience. This involves investing money in three areas: Benchmarking, Quality Functional Deployment Efforts and Concurrent Engineering/6 Sigma training. Investing in one or more of these TQM areas will reduce administrative overhead, carrying costs, and the research and development time cycle while it increases the impact of promotion and sales investments. Investing the "right amount" in TQM initiatives is important. If you spend too little or too much, your returns on a per dollar invested basis diminish. A TQM tutorial is available at www.capsim.com that further describes this process.

Technology

Many production processes have become automated and robotics has become a significant factor in manufacturing throughout the world. From the early, simple machines to intelligent machines of today, robotics has changed the face of industry from automotive manufactures to food processing. Machines and robotic equipment may reduce the manpower required in the production process. Although these machines may be an initial expense, their ongoing use can reduce labor expenses due to the efficiencies they offer. Good planning is required to make certain that the automation process accomplishes the desired goals. This involves a thorough assessment of the costs required, the savings and benefits that may be realized, and the degree of fit within the organization and production process.

In Foundation™

The production of each product takes place in a single plant. The "first shift" capacity is the number of units that can be produced on an assembly line in a single year. A second shift is capable of doubling this figure with overtime wages of 50% more than that of the first shift. For example, if your first shift has the capacity to produce 800 products each year, your second shift can produce that same amount for a total annual production capacity of 1,600 units. However, products produced on the second shift require overtime wages and are therefore more expensive products. There are ways to reduce the dependency on overtime. One option is automation. The production process can be more highly automated and therefore decrease labor hours needed. A second option is to expand the capacity of the plant to be able to produce more products each year without requiring as much overtime. There is a one year lag between the purchase of automation and capacity before it is available for use. Therefore, advanced planning is required.

Improving Productivity

A healthy economy often correlates with consistent improvement in productivity. A common measure of productivity is expressed in dollar of output per hour worked. Production faces the standard challenges of increasing labor, material and opportunity costs. It also must address the impact of uncertain world events, technological change and the global labor market. This is combined with the consumer trend demanding higher quality standards as companies work to improve the output based on required resources.

Review and Discussion Questions

1. Discuss the primary resources involved in the production process.
2. What does "economies of scale" mean and why is that concept relevant in the production process?
3. What are the key advantages of JIT?
4. Can inventory control systems, such as the JIT technique, be applied to the operation of a service-based business?
5. What benefits does TQM offer an organization?
6. What does benchmarking accomplish?
7. How does supply chain management impact the production process?
8. What are the potential benefits of effectively managing quality control?
9. What do you consider to be the single most challenging aspect of the production process?

An Introduction to Business

Chapter 6

Business and Society:
The legal and regulatory system

The private enterprise system requires laws to make corrections when markets do not produce the outcomes most desired by the people in a society.

Key terms to look for:

- Administrative law
- Agency
- Arbitration
- Civil law
- Common law
- Contract law
- Criminal law
- Expressed warranty
- Fraud
- Limited warranty
- Mediation
- Statutory law
- Tort

Business and Society: The legal and regulatory system

Our society has agreed to live by a set of rules or laws that insure these conditions exist and are protected. These standards are set by the customs of the society or through the action of the government, which acts as the agent for the society. While the law establishes the private enterprise system, it also corrects for the times when markets fail or when markets do not produce the outcomes most desired by the people in a society.

We discussed the four conditions required for the private enterprise system to work:
1. Right to private property
2. Right to keep profits
3. Freedom of Choice
4. Fair competition

These four conditions, necessary for the private enterprise system to function, are established in different bodies of law. When these conditions exist, competition for transactions in markets will create pressure for innovation, pressure for low prices, and result in an efficient allocation of goods. As a society, we value these outcomes.

Freedom of choice is established in the Constitution of the United States as an underlying principle upon which the country was founded. It does not serve a useful purpose to review the body of laws guaranteeing choice.

The right to *private property* and the right to *keep profits* are defined in a body of property law. **Property law** establishes the rights of a person to own, use, transfer and capture the economic value of different kinds of property. It recognizes that property can be *tangible* (has a physical existence like a car) and *intangible* (stock in a corporation or a trademark). Property law establishes:

- **Real property**: Real estate and everything attached to it
- **Personal property**: Property other than real property
- **Intellectual property**: Property generated by a person's creative activities. Copyrights protect the ownership of property such as books, music, and software. Patents give an inventor the exclusive right to exploit an invention for a period of time. A trademark provides legal protection to a created identity or a brands. This may be based upon a name, a mark or a symbol.

Fair competition is established in a wide variety of law and regulation. In general, fair competition is broadly established in laws that prevent businesses from
- Restraining trade and monopolizing markets (Sherman Antitrust Act)
- Price discrimination, tying, exclusive agreements that substantially lessen competition (Clayton Act).

All areas of law that influence business practice contribute to our shared definition of fairness. Examples are the laws and regulations that establish standards of conducts in

78

negotiating contracts with a company's buyers or suppliers, providing information (advertising) to consumers, providing information to potential investors, negotiating with employees or their representatives.

Contract Law

The heart of the private enterprise system is the transaction or a mutual agreement of exchange. Virtually every transaction is carried out by means of a contract. A contract is a mutual agreement between two or more parties whose terms are enforceable in court. A contract does not have to be written. It is any agreement that meets three criteria which are called elements and include:

1. *Voluntary agreement*. The offer and acceptance have to be freely and knowingly made and it is not a contract if any party uses fraud or force to come to agreement.

2. *Consideration*. To be a contract, the agreement to exchange must involve something of economic value (money, goods, or services). Therefore, the word consideration is another term for "money."

3. *Contractual capacity*. To be a contract, both parties must have a legal ability to enter into the contract. Individuals who are minors (under the age of 18), mentally unstable, retarded, insane, or intoxicated lacking the capacity to enter into a legal contract.

The failure to live up to the terms agreed upon in a contract is called breach of contract. If arbitration is not used. a court can order the terms of the contract to be met and damages to be paid if the breach resulted in monetary damages.

Sources of Law

How did the "rules" of our society come into existence? There are three sources:

Statutory law. Written laws established by federal, state, county, or city governments.

Common law. Unwritten laws that are established by judicial decisions; the US inherited this law from England

Administrative law. Regulations established by administrative agencies

Dispute Resolution

Whenever there are individuals acting in their own best interest, there will be conflict. As standards of behavior are established, there will be disputes over whether specific behaviors meet the standards. There are two kinds of disputes:

1. Disputes between the government; and,

2. Individual and disputes between two individuals. *("Individuals" are any form of private party and can include different kinds of businesses).*

A dispute between the government and an individual over whether behavior meets the set standards is a matter of *criminal law*. Violation of criminal law is called a crime and may be punished by fines and/or imprisonment. A dispute between two individuals is considered a matter of *civil law*. Violations of civil law may result in fines but not imprisonment.

Violations of criminal law are resolved through the court system. Each level of government (on federal, state and city levels for example) has its own courts to resolve violations of the laws that they establish. *Trial courts* determine the facts of a case, the laws that pertain, and apply the law to resolve the dispute. If either party feels that the law was misinterpreted or misapplied, they can appeal the decision in an *appellate court*. Court judgments are binding and are enforced through the power of the government

When two individuals have a dispute, they may initiate a *lawsuit* where one individual takes another to court using civil laws. Civil disputes are initiated and resolved through lawsuits. Lawsuits are the main remedy for business disputes. Like criminal law, they are resolved in trial and appellate courts.

Legal Options

The United States is a litigious society. This is a sophisticated way of saying we sue each other often. As a result of this demand and long delays in our court systems, alternative methods of dispute resolution are gaining popularity that typically are faster and more cost effective than litigation through the traditional court system.

Arbitration is a form of dispute resolution where the parties submit their case to a neutral third party called an arbitrator. This person decides how the dispute will be resolved and acts somewhat like a judge in the process. In most cases, arbitration is binding and requires the parties to accept the legally binding and enforceable solution. Either party may appeal the arbitrator's decision to a court but the court will generally not change the arbitrator's findings but will decide only whether the arbitrator acted properly.

Mediation is a form of negotiated resolution using a third party mediator to help reach an agreement. A neutral negotiator helps the two parties negotiate a settlement. Typically the mediator meets with each side separately until both sides agree to a settlement. Unlike arbitration, mediation is non-binding and neither side has the power of the courts to enforce the settlement. The dissatisfied party can take this case to court. In other words, the mediator functions more like a counselor than a judge and the parties do not have to accept the mediator's decision.

Agency

Agency law allows an individual to assign the power to act and enter into agreements to another person. The two parties (the principal and the agent) enter into an *agency agreement*. The *principal* is the person who wishes to have a specific task accomplished and the **agent** is the one who acts on the principal's behalf. *Power of attorney* is a legal document that authorizes a person to act as another's agent. A *Partnership Agreement* establishes a business partnership (form of organization) and creates mutual agency for the partners to the company.

Bankruptcy

If an individual (or business) can not meet its contractual obligations, it can declare bankruptcy as an option of last resort. Bankruptcy, or legal insolvency, asks a court to declare an individual or company unable to meet its contractual obligations and release them from those obligations. The assets of the person or company declared bankrupt are sold to meet as much of the contractual obligation as possible. There are different kinds of bankruptcy:

- **Chapter 7** requires that the business be dissolved and assets liquidated
- **Chapter 11** temporarily frees the business from its obligations while it reorganizes and works out a court-approved plan for meeting its obligations
- **Chapter 13** is like Chapter 11, except it is limited to individuals

Uniform Commercial Code

Because laws governing business practice can come from many sources, the states (except Louisiana) have adopted a consistent set of statutory laws that simplify commerce called the Uniform Commercial Code (UCC). As an example, the UCC has a section covering sales agreements, which are of course, contracts. The UCC addresses the rights of buyers and sellers, transfers of ownership, the legal assumption of risk, and warranties. A warranty defines the terms that the seller will honor. All sales are covered by an ***implied warranty*** that allows the buyer to assume that:

- The seller has clear title to the product (it has not been stolen);
- The product will perform the function for which it was produced and sold; and,
- It will perform as advertised.

An "***expressed warranty***" covers any additional terms the seller will honor. An automobile manufacturer might offer a 5-year, 50,000 mile warranty on a vehicle during which they will fix any defects in the car.

TORTS AND FRAUD

As a society, we expect that the conduct of business will not "wrong" or harm others.

Fraud is a criminal act in which one party in a transaction hurts another by purposefully deceiving or manipulating them. If a "travel agency" sold you a vacation package but never intended to deliver the plane tickets, that is fraud. If a hospital bills your insurance company for services they did not provide, that is fraud. A criminal act and fraud convictions can result in imprisonment and fines.

A ***tort*** is a civil wrong (and includes all "wrongs" that are not breach of contract) in which one party through action or inaction causes harm to another. If a UPS driver loses control of a truck and causes injury to a person (or their property), that person can sue the driver and the company for damages.

An important part of tort law is ***product liability***, which establishes a business's legal responsibility to be diligent (not negligent) in the design, production, sale, and consumption of products. Liability often relies on the concept of what a *reasonable person* might expect to happen when using a product. A reasonable person would expect a kitchen knife to be sharp and could not sue if he or she were cut while using it. A reasonable person would not expect a kitchen knife to break or separate from its handle in normal use and could sue if this happened and an injury or damage resulted.

FEDERAL ADMINISTRATIVE AGENCIES

Governments can pass a law that sets up an administrative agency that establishes operating rules (regulations) to guide business practices. Many agencies also have the power to resolve disputes involving their regulations. In these disputes, an administrative law judge decides the issues in a "hearing" not a trial. Most agencies are established to regulate the practices in a specific industry.

Cross-industry Agencies:

- **Federal Trade Commission** (FTC): business practice; false and deceptive advertising, labeling and pricing.
- **Consumer Product Safety Commission** (CPSC): consumer safety
- **Occupational Safety and Health Administration** (OSHA): worker safety issues
- **Equal Employment Opportunity Commission** (EEOC): employment discrimination
- **Environmental Protection Agency** (EPA): pollution standards

Industry Specific Agencies

- **Food and Drug Administration** (FDA): foods and drugs
- **Interstate Commerce Commission** (ICC): rail, trucks, buses, ships
- **Federal Communications Commission** (FCC) wire, radio, TV
- **Federal Energy Regulatory Commission** (FERC): electricity, gas
- **Federal Aviation Administration** (FAA): airline industry
- **Federal Highway Administration** (FHA): vehicle safety
- **Securities and Exchange Commission** (SEC): corporate securities trading

Review and Discussion Questions

1. What are the requirements of a business contract and why are these important?
2. What are the differences between a criminal and civil law?
3. Describe the concept of agency and how it may be applied.
4. What is the primary reason for the existence of government and other regulatory organizations in business?
5. What are the two types of warranties and how do they vary?
6. What are the dispute resolution options and how might they impact legal options?
7. For what reasons might a person's contractual capacity be limited or nonexistent?

Chapter 7

Forms of Business Organization

Business owners determine the best form of the business ownership based on the number of owners, anticipated risk, expected profitability, and the potential future value of the firm.

Key terms to look for:

- Bylaws
- Common stock
- Corporation
- Limited liability company
- Mutual agency
- Partnership
- Preferred stock
- S-corporation
- Sole proprietorship

Forms of Business Organization

When a business is established, the owners must decide on the form of the business ownership. The choice relate to the number of owners, the level of personal protection they seek, and the anticipated profitability, risk and potential value of the firm. The organizational forms most commonly used by businesses in the United States fall into four general categories:

Sole proprietorship
Partnership
Corporation
Limited liability company

To understand the differences between these forms (and the advantages and disadvantages of each), you should know:

- How is each type of legal organization set up? *(starting an organization)*
- Who owns the business? *(control)*
- Who is responsible if the business fails or has losses? *(liability)*
- How long does each type of organization last, and how does the owner sell the business? *(life of and sale of company)*
- How are the profits and losses of the business taxed? *(taxes)*

SOLE PROPRIETORSHIP

This is the simplest and most common form of business organization. Its primary advantage is its ease of formation; its most important disadvantages are:

It can have only one owner.
The owner is individually responsible for all losses of the business.

Starting a Sole Proprietorship

You can start a sole proprietorship simply by beginning to conduct your business. You should set up a system to keep track of your business's finances and keep records of all revenues and expenses. A sole proprietorship is usually operated under the name of the individual owner, although you can choose another name. You should check with local government offices for information about licenses and permits. Examples include business licenses, zoning occupancy permits and tax registrations.

Management and Control

If you create a sole proprietorship, all the assets of the business are owned directly by you. A sole proprietorship may be owned by only one person. The owner controls the business. You may hire employees to help manage your business, but you will have legal responsibility for the decisions made by your employees.

Liability

In a sole proprietorship, the owner and the business are legally the same. As the owner, you will have unlimited personal responsibility for your business's liabilities. For example, if your business cannot pay its loans, the bank can take action against you individually against both the business's assets and your personal assets, including your bank account, car or house.

The Life and Sale of a Sole Proprietorship

A sole proprietorship exists as long as its owner is alive and wants to continue the business. When the owner dies, the assets and liabilities of the business become part of the owner's estate. A sole proprietor is free to sell all or any part of the assets of the business.

Taxes

Because there is no legal difference between the person and the business, the business's income (minus allowable expenses) are reported on the owner's individual tax return and taxed at individual tax rates. No separate federal income tax return is required of the sole proprietor.

Advantages	Disadvantages
Inexpensive to start	Unlimited personal liability
Simple to run	Ownership is limited to one person
Single (simple) taxation on profits	Most limited access to capital

PARTNERSHIPS

In the most general form, a partnership is created when two or more individuals agree to create a business and to jointly own the assets, be responsible for the liabilities, share the profits and losses. There are many different ways to structure a partnership and you can limit a partners "participation" (and liability) in the partnership agreement (get a good lawyer to help). The advantages of a partnership are that they can have more than one owner; and so access to more capital and managerial talent. The disadvantage is that the general partners are personally responsible for the losses and other obligations of the business and their partner's business decisions.

Starting a partnership

You can start a general partnership by agreeing with one or more individuals to jointly own and share the profits of a business. You can form a partnership with other individuals, other partnerships, or corporations. You can have as many partners as you want.

A general partnership is usually established with a ***partnership agreement*** that addresses:
- What each partner will contribute to the business.
- How business decisions will be made.
- How profits and losses will be shared.
- When profits will be distributed to the partners.
- How long the partnership will exist and under what conditions it changes (What will happens when a partner dies, becomes disabled, or stops working).

If you want to limit the participation and liability of a partner, the limits would be established in a partnership agreement. The law assumes a "general" participation unless specific statutory requirements are met, so be sure to have a lawyer review the agreement

A partnership often operates under the names of the partners. Some states require partnerships to file partnership certificates, often with the secretary of state's office. If the partner's names are not used, you may need to file a "doing business as" form. You should check with local government offices for information about licenses and permits. The partnership should set up a system to keep track of the business's finances and keep records of all revenues and expenses so the partners know whether there are profits and how the accrue to the individual partner.

Management and Control

The partnership agreement defines the percentage of the business and profits each partner will own. Be careful, the law might assume that each partner will have an equal claim on the assets of the business, its profits, and its liabilities. Most partnership agreements are negotiated on the principal of a proportional claim based on the cumulative investments of the partner.

Mutual agency

Partnerships are based on the concept of mutual agency. The partnership is held responsible for the decisions and behavior of each partner (this is an example of "a chain is only as strong as the weakest link" principle). Any partner can bind the partnership to contracts or legal obligations without the approval of the other partners. Any partner can expose the partnership to criminal or civil actions.

The partnership agreement should specify who controls and manages the business. Again, in the absence of a specific agreement, all general partners have equal control and equal management rights over the business. This means that all of the partners must consent and agree to partnership decisions.

If the purpose of limiting the partnership is to limit the liability of a partner, then the limited partner must have limited managerial control. The premise is that partners are responsible, and protection from responsibility can not be given to active decision makers.

Unlimited Liability of General Partners

A general partnership has some characteristics of a legal entity that is separate from its owners. For instance a partnership can own property and conduct business. However, the general partners have unlimited personal liability and are in an agency relationship with all other partners. All of the partners are liable together and each general partner is individually liable for any and all of the obligations of the partnership. This means that a partner could borrow money in the name of the partnership and the creditor could require you individually to pay the money. If you cannot pay back the money your partner borrowed, your personal assets might be used (your home, car, etc) to meet this obligation.

Limited Liability of Limited Partners

Limited partners do not have personal liability for the business of the partnership. Limited partners risk only their investment (or specified contributions) to the partnership.

The Life and Sale of a Partnership

A partnership last as long as (1) the partners agree it will or (2) all of the general partners remain in the partnership. In general, what happens when a partner dies or leaves the partnership should be specified in the partnership agreement. If the partnership dissolves, the assets of the partnership are sold, the liabilities are settled, and the remainder distributed to the partners. The partnership agreement should state whether a partner can sell his or her share, under what conditions (does it require unanimous consent of the partners); and how the share of the assets and profits of the partnership will be determined.

Taxes

The partnership itself incurs no taxes although it files a partnership tax return for informational purposes. Each partner pays personal taxes on his or her share of the business income. A partner may be required to pay tax on income without having received any cash dispersal from the partnership. Investing the professional advice of lawyer or accountant is worthwhile.

Advantages	Disadvantages
Access to capital of more than one person	Mutual agency
Access to talent/ energy of more than one person	Unlimited personal liability
Few legal formalities	Can not sell without consent of partners
Avoids double taxation	Dissolves at death of partner

Subchapter S-corporations

Subchapter S-corporations are a special form of a partnership that is referred to as a corporation. S-corporation places some limits on the type and number of shareholders. Sub S-corporations have to meet the following requirements:

- The corporation has no more than 35 total shareholders;
- The corporation has only one class of stock;
- All of the shareholders are U.S. residents, either citizens or resident aliens;
- All of the shareholders are individuals (i.e., no corporations or other entities own the stock)
- The corporation operates on a calendar year financial basis.

If you can meet these criteria, then your Subchapter S-corporation is not liable for "double taxation." That is, the Sub-S-corporation does not pay taxes on the income generated by the business. Instead, the income or losses are passed through to the individual shareholders and reported on their tax returns. The income or losses are divided among the shareholders based upon the percentage of stock of the corporation that they own.

CORPORATION

A corporation is a separate legal entity that exists independently of its owners, referred to as stockholders. This is a major advantage of the corporation because it limits stockholder liability. They are not personally responsible for the losses of the business beyond their initial investment.

Starting a corporation

Creating a corporation is the most complex of all the business entities. If you decide to form a corporation, you have to follow the formal requirements of state in which you are incorporating. Most states require the owners to file Articles of Incorporation or Certificate of Incorporation, with the appropriate state office, again most commonly with the secretary of state's office. In general, these articles include:

- The corporate name
- The number of shares of stock the corporation is authorized to issue
- The number of shares of stock each of the owners will buy.
- The each owner's contribution to obtain these shares of stock.
- The business of the corporation.
- The management structure of the corporation (directors and officers)

There is a fee for filing the corporate documents and an annual fee for keeping the corporation in existence

The corporation also needs bylaws or the rules by which the corporation is run. *Bylaws* are general guidelines for managing a firm and specify such activities as annual stockholder meetings, meetings of the board of directors, the number, titles, selection, and responsibilities of each officer.

Because the corporate business entity is separate from its owners, it has to set up its own record keeping system. The assets and liabilities, the profits and losses are owned by the corporation and not by the shareholders.

Corporations may operate in states and countries in addition to the state in which they incorporated. Corporations are categorized into three areas:

Domestic Corporation — Operates in the state in which it was incorporated

Foreign Corporation — Incorporated in one state but has operations in another and therefore, the "other" state considers it a *foreign corporation*.

Alien Corporation — Operates in a country in which it was not incorporated, it is considered an *alien corporation* in that country.

Management and Control

The owners, or the shareholders of the corporation, have to vote directly on certain major decisions such as amendments to the articles of incorporation, dissolving the corporation. For most decisions that do not change the nature or character of the organization, the owners elect a group of individuals to act as the board of directors. Usually, each share of stock gets one vote. Those who hold a majority of the shares have ultimate control over the corporation. Shareholders can elect themselves to the board of directors.

The board of directors is responsible to provide guidance to the executive management team of the corporation. Directors may be paid for their services, although it is not required. The board of directors determine who fills the role of the key officers within the corporation, who in turn, are responsible for running the day-to-day business.

If you own stock in a corporation, you may be paid a dividend or cash distribution on the stock you own. A dividend must be paid equally to all shares of common stock and is usually expressed as an amount per share, such as "$5 per share." The board of directors typically decide whether dividends shall be paid, how much and when.

Liability

Because a corporation is a separate legal entity, creditors of the corporation only have a claim against the assets of the corporation for payment. Individual shareholders are not personally liable for the losses of the business beyond their initial investment. This limited liability makes investment in a corporation very attractive.

The Life and Sale of a Corporation

The corporation, as a separate legal entity, lasts as long as its shareholders decide it should. For most practical purposes a corporation's life is considered perpetual, meaning forever. It can be stated that a corporation will continue in perpetuity. The sale of ownership rights in a corporation is easy: it is the sale of shares of stock. Corporations can issue two types of stock: preferred and common.

- *Preferred stock* conveys special ownership rights- they have a "preferred" claim on profits of the company. This claim is in the form of a preferred dividend (if there is enough net income, the preferred stockholders are guaranteed a dividend). Preferred stockholders do not have a say in how the company is run and do not have voting rights in the board of director elections.

- *Common stock* conveys no special privileges with respect to the profits of the company but does convey voting rights in the corporation.

Shares of stock can be purchased from current owners (who wish to sell) or from the authorized and issued shares of the corporation. These transactions generally occur in the stock markets of the world.

Taxes

As a separate legal entity, the corporation must file its own income tax returns and pay taxes on its profits. The corporation must report all income it has received from its business and may deduct certain expenses it has paid in conducting its business.

Double Taxation

In addition to corporate income taxes, dividends paid to shareholders are regarded as personal income and the shareholder must pay tax on that income. This is why there is said to be a "double tax" on corporations. Based on laws that are now being reviewed at the federal level, double taxation for corporations may change in the near future.

Advantages	Disadvantages
Limited liability	Costly to set up and maintain
Easy to transfer ownership to others	Can lose control of organization to larger shareholders
Easy to raise money and add additional owners	Double taxation

LIMITED LIABILITY COMPANY

The newest business entity is a Limited Liability Company, or LLC, and was introduced as a response to our litigious business climate. This is a type of general partnership that possesses the favorable feature of a general partnership with limited liability for the partners like a corporation. It offers the simplicity of a partnership with the legal protection of a corporation. Although corporations, including S-corporations, provide liability protection, various rules may limit the liability of some partners that an LLC is not subject to. An LLC is created according to the laws of the state where the business is located.

Advantages	Disadvantages
Limited personal liability	Can not sell without consent of partners
Does not require strict government reporting	Can lose control of organization to larger shareholders
Avoids double taxation	Dissolves at death of partner

Selecting the "Right" Form of Business

No single form of business ownership is ideal for all. Individuals starting a business can easily begin as a sole proprietorship and then transition from there. When two are more are involved, a sole proprietorship is not a fit and they need to look at the other options. If there are "risk" concerns regarding the nature of the business, then an LLC or Corporation may be the best choices to consider. An attorney and a CPA are good advisors to consult with regarding the best business entity.

Review and Discussion Questions

1. What are the advantages and disadvantages of a sole proprietorship, a partnership, an LLC and a corporation?
2. What is the relationship between a common stockholder and the board of directors?
3. Which of the business organizations restricts the number of owners?
4. Which organization offers the optimal situation for raising capital?
5. What do the articles of partnership include?
6. What are the benefits of an LLC versus a partnership or a corporation—why would an organization make that choice?
7. Pressure has been placed on the federal government to change the tax laws for corporations. How might that change the value of being a stockholder?

Chapter 8

Developing a Business Plan

The value is not in the document itself,
but in what you learn as you create it.

Key terms to look for:

- Executive summary
- Mission statement
- Proforma statements
- SWOT analysis
- Vision statement

91

Developing a Business Plan

In order to create sound business decisions, you must first have a cohesive plan that supports clearly defined success measurements. Your product positioning, marketing, production, and finance plans should all align strategically in support of your objective.

Business plans may be generated in many different formats. Much depends on to whom the plan is designed to appeal. For example, a business plan designed to inform employees of the company's long-term strategic intents may be promulgated differently from one intended to appeal to bank lenders and venture capitalists. Regardless of format, there are four major phases to business planning:

- Determine the current state of the industry and the market (Situation Analysis). Identify SWOT (Strengths, Weaknesses, Opportunities, and Threats).

- Set forth a strategic vision for the company (make sure it aligns with your success measurements).

- Determine the specific tactics within each of the company's functional elements (Research and Development, Marketing, Production, and Finance) that you believe will best support the strategic vision.

- Monitor progress by establishing benchmarks and conducting competitor analysis comparisons.

The following is a sample business plan format:

I.   **EXECUTIVE SUMMARY**
Summarizes the main themes of your strategic vision in a few paragraphs — what the company will do and why. Broadly describe how you intend to gain competitive advantage.

II..   **MISSION STATEMENT**
Captures the primary goal of the organization describing "why" it exists.

III.   **VISION STATEMENT** — *a newer addition to the standard business plan*
A brief summary (usually one paragraph) of company philosophy — easily understood by employees and customers.

IV.   **RESEARCH AND DEVELOPMENT**
Detail plans for product repositioning and new product introduction. The research and development section of a business plans answers these questions:

- Which - if any - of your existing products will be repositioned, and where? Which will be phased out?

- Will you introduce new products? If so, how many, when and in which market segment(s) will they be positioned?

- What will you do with the products' MTBF ratings, which have a direct impact on material costs?

V. MARKETING

Detail your plans for pricing, promotion, and selling tactics addressing these questions:

- Will you price above, at, or below industry averages? If you are going to price high, how will you justify those prices? If you select a low price strategy, how will you keep margins large enough to turn a profit?

- Will pricing strategies be different for each market segment?

- Will you spend a lot on advertising and sales, or very little? What do you hope to achieve with your advertising expenditures? Do you want 100% customer awareness, or will 50% suit your needs? Are you a cost conscious company or are you willing to spend whatever is necessary to be well known by every potential customer?

VI. PRODUCTION

Describe investment and or liquidation plans for your factories by addressing these questions:

- Will you be better off investing in automation, capacity, or both?

- Will you keep overtime to a minimum, or will you run a lot of overtime as an alternative to capacity expansions?

- Which of the factories will you liquidate — if any— and will you do it gradually or all at once?

- When launching new products, will you build expensive highly automated factories or low-tech labor intensive plants?

VII. FINANCE

Detail plans for raising capital, debt, and stock and dividend policies by considering the following:

- Will you raise capital through short-term debt, long-term debt, stock issues, factory liquidation, or a combination of these means?

- Will you be fairly conservative and maintain a substantial cash reserve to stave off high interest emergency loans, or will you aggressively seek to make every dollar work for maximum return?

Fundamentally, a business plan allows you to create more objectivity around a business idea by looking at it holistically for problems and pitfalls. More importantly, this objectivity provides an opportunity to find innovation solutions.

A successful business plan effectively communicates the market need, the product and/or service solution, projected profitability and who you are and why you believe you can make it work.

Altitude and Audience
Altitude is the respective level at which you research and write. It is characterized by the level of detail you are working at. Research should be as close to the ground as possible. The plan should be written at an altitude that allows the reader to quickly grasp your plan without loosing the innovative aspects of the solution.

One challenge is keeping your altitude consistent, and at an elevation that gives the reader enough information, but does not overwhelm or distract them. Knowing your audience helps. Normally your audience is educated, but unfamiliar with your business. Avoid abbreviations, lingo and trade slang, both from your industry and from your business.

Executive Summary
The executive summary provides a brief overview of the plan that lies ahead. It captures key highlights in an orderly manner that describes the venture and creates interest for the reader to proceed. It is a miniature business plan that should convey:
1. The business concept (solution)
2. Market (need)
3. How you plan to meet it (profitability)
4. Make key assertions

Conversely, the executive summary is not:
- An abstract of the business plan
- An introduction to the business plan
- A preface
- A random collection of highlights

94

The executive summary is the opportunity to make a bold statement, without providing the justification contained in the more detailed plan. Remember, everything you state in the executive summary must be supported and proved in the rest of the plan.

Market (Customer) Analysis

Although your product or service will determine industry competitors and customers, the Market Analysis should be focused on the market and the conditions, not your solution. Clearly establishing the market sets the background for the solution.

Industry Analysis

This section demonstrates an understanding of direct competitors, including substitutes for your product or service. If you are entering a new or expanding market niche, which competitors are likely to enter? The number, size, and history of the competitors will drive your strategy for entry and growth.

Identify your key competitors (or groups), their current share in the market, and how important the market is to them. Useful tools for characterizing the degree of competitiveness in the market are SWOT, TOWS and Porter's Five Forces analyses. This type of information can concisely be presented in tables. Noting key competitors is important, but extensive data belongs in the appendix.

Key parameters of an industry analysis include:

- Number of competitors
- Nature of competitors
- Growth of the market
- Major customer groups

Target Market

Who will be buying your product? Will you distribute to businesses in a business-to-business (B2B) arrangement, or consumers in a business-to-consumer (B2C) arrangement? The nature of your customer will drive marketing and sales efforts. Clearly describe the unmet need you will be solving. The remainder of the plan should be describing how you can meet this need better than anyone else based upon:

- Distinguishing characteristics
- Primary target market size
- Expected market penetration (share)
- Pricing, margins and expected discounts (or rebates)
- How you will identify your target market
- Marketing media
- Customer purchasing cycle
- Secondary market attributes (why are they secondary market?)

Company Description

In one or two brief paragraphs, summarize:

- Nature of your company
- Market need you are meeting
- How you plan to meet the need
- Distinctive competencies you have, or will gain

This information can become redundant, so work at keeping your comments concise.

Product and/or Service Descriptions

Provide a clear description of how your customer will view and handle your product. Pictures and Diagrams save words, and keep your plan interesting. Items like product specification sheets are best put into the appendices. The plan should briefly describe:

- Expected life-cycles,
- Add-on or next generation products
- Intellectual protection (patents, trademarks, etc.)
- Planned areas of research and development
- How does your solution compare to your competitors?

Marketing & Sales Activities

Describe your strategies for making your target customer aware of your product, and how you will accomplish the following:

- Market penetration
- Growth
- Distribution
- Communication
- Sales force
- Sales activities

Timeline (Milestones)

A clear timeline with milestones demonstrates you understand the requirements (and hurdles) for succeeding. These milestones should correspond with the funds required.

Operations

Operations are often left out or overemphasized. Show you have a clear understanding of how your product or service will be produced, without going through all of the details. The strategy for operations must be congruent with your market. A differentiated production strategy in a low-cost market will quickly be dismissed. If you are in early stages of development, explain the criteria you must meet to be successful.

Management and Ownership

Key elements of any business are the character and drive of management, how the company is structured, and who owns it. The management team and advisor are the foundation of all successful businesses. Leadership, innovation, and determination can make or break a business. The management and advisory teams establish your credibility.

Management Team

Include a brief description of your key players and their roles. Just as important, identify the skills and experience you are missing and how and when you plan to fill them. The timing of additions to the management team should match with growth expectations. A chart of your management structure is an excellent way to show relationships.

Board of Advisors

The best source of information and advise is from people who are already in the industry you plan to enter, have had experience their, or have experience serving your competitors. People who have established their own businesses will be able to quickly identify problems with your plan and solution. Do not just list these individuals, USE them. Surround yourself with people who are experienced where you are weak. The plan should reflect their input, so keep your description concise:

- Advisors name
- Area of expertise they provide
- Brief background

As a company matures, these individuals may become part of a board of trustees. With a more formal board, position titles and past contributions also become essential information.

Funds Required and Their Use

This is another brief but essential section that should convey:

- Current funding needs
- How (or for what) they be used
- Expected return for the investor (loan, equity, equity or convertible debt)

In addition, what are future funding requirements? Investors are compensated by the level of risk they take. The earlier in a business, the more you will have to give up. By staging funding, the entrepreneur does not have to give up as much. The last part of funding requirements is relaying the strategies for exiting or repaying your investors.

Financial Data

Financials can have two parts, historic and future. Operational businesses should have a clear financial history. The biggest question is, who created it, a book keeper or a CPA, and what level of involvement did the CPA have. This establishes your credibility. Depending on your exit strategy, third party auditing and certification may be necessary.

Pro forma (or future) financial projects should be an objective assessment that includes all of the milestones and strategies you have outlined in your plan. Every change in your business plan should be reflected in your financials. This is why the financials are often frustrating, and the last thing to be nailed down. The executive summary along with amount and timing of required funds (not their use) should be the only aspects of your plan that are completed after your financials.

Obtaining funding requires establishing the value of your business and the value the funding will provide. Four things that determine the value are:

1. Amount of capital already invested
2. Intellectual Protection
3. Value of Assets held
4. The business potential

One way to determine today's value is to determine a reasonable future value, and then discount back to find today's value. The discount factor is related to the level of risk associated with the business succeeding (not with current interest rates). The next two sections explain the expectations of investors at various stages of business growth, and two ways to determine the future value of a company.

Appendices and Exhibits

"Should this be in the plan?" If that is a question you find yourself asking, it may be better to include it in the appendices or an exhibit. Review the appendix to make sure these additions that support your plan and are referred to in the body of the plan itself. If not, you may want to keep the information for your own reference, but take it out of the plan.

The following, in an order that flows with your plan, should be considered for the appendix[1]:

- Market Studies
- Patents
- Pertinent Published Information
- Pictures of Products
- Pro Forma Financial Statements
- Professional References
- Resumes of Key Managers
- Significant Contracts

---

[1] "Outline for a Business Plan: A Proven Approach for Entrepreneurs Only," Ernst & Young LLP, 1997

98

An Introduction to Business

About Mission Statements and Foundations

An organization's mission is its reason for existing. A "mission statement" describes the business in terms of goods, markets, services, and client needs. The "mission statement" should define an organization's ultimate strategic intent for profitability, growth, market share, and building competitive advantage.

Foundation™ firms may develop and execute any strategy (or none at all—though that is not advisable). Basic strategies include:

- Overall cost leader
- Cost leader with low-tech focus
- Cost leader with product life-cycle focus
- Differentiator
- Differentiator with high-tech focus
- Differentiator with product life-cycle focus

Your Foundation™ Business Plan

The business plan that your develop will have to be appropriate to the current situation of your company. It will give the reader a sense of what your business is about.

To create a business plan for your Foundation company, you need to:
- Develop or state your strategy and mission statement.
- Outline your company's marketing, production, and financial plans and actions.
- Describe your current condition – good or bad – to communicate key facts about your business.
- Translate that information into a cohesive documents that "tells the story" about your business.
- Create and executive summary that "engages" the reader to want to learn more about your business.

99

OVERALL COST LEADER

An overall cost leader will attempt to be the low-cost producer in both segments of the market. It will have good profit margins on all sales while keeping prices low for price-sensitive customers.

Firm Profile:

- More likely to reposition products than introduce new ones to the market
- Capacity improvements are unlikely to be undertaken (may run overtime instead)
- Automation may be pursued to increase margins
- Investments will be financed with debt and/or stock issues
- Tends to spend less on promotion and sales
- Focus on Market Share, Profits, and Stock Price

COST LEADER WITH LOW TECH FOCUS

A Low Tech focused cost leader seeks to dominate the price sensitive market segments. Its aim is to set prices below all competitors — and still be profitable.

Firm Profile:

Multiple product lines in the Low Tech segment
Invests heavily in automation
Spends moderately on advertising to cost sensitive customers (sales people have more than one product to pitch to prospects)
Investments financed with debt and/or stock issues
Focus on ROS, ROE, and Profits

COST LEADER WITH PRODUCT LIFE-CYCLE FOCUS

A product life-cycle focused cost leader will seek to minimize costs through efficiency and expertise. Products will be allowed to age and change in appeal from High Tech to Low Tech buyers.

Firm Profile:

Low R&D spending (very little repositioning & new product every 2-3 years)
Invests in automation early in the product's life-cycle
Moderate spending on promotion and sales
Focus on ROE, ROS, and Profits

DIFFERENTIATOR

A differentiator will seek to create maximum awareness and brand equity. It wants to be well known as a maker of high quality/highly desirable products.

Firm Profile:

High R&D spending to keep products fresh
Maintains a presence in both market segments
Spends heavily on advertising and sales to create maximum awareness and accessibility
Prices tend to be higher
Focus on Market Share, Profits, and Stock Price

DIFFERENTIATOR WITH HIGH-TECH FOCUS

A High Tech differentiator seeks to be known far and wide as the top producer of the best performing state-of-the-art products.

Firm Profile:

- Multiple product lines in the High Tech Segment
- Minimum focus in the other segment
- High promotion and sales investments to create optimal awareness and accessibility
- High R&D expenditures to continually introduce new product lines and keep existing products fresh
- Unlikely to invest in increased automation or production capacity
- Focus on ROA, Asset Turnover, and ROE

DIFFERENTIATOR WITH PRODUCT LIFE-CYCLE FOCUS

A product life-cycle differentiator seeks to be well-known as a top producer of good performing products in each of the targeted segments.

Firm Profile:

Multiple product lines in both segments

- High promotion and sales investments to create maximum awareness and accessibility
- High R&D expenditures to continually reposition product lines to keep them fresh
- Unlikely to invest in increased automation or production capacity
- Focus on ROA, Stock Price, and Asset Turnover

Glossary

An online business glossary that you may find useful is:
http://www.nytimes.com/library/financial/glossary/bfglosa.htm

A

Accessibility The availability of the product for the customer to gain access to. The higher the accessibility, the more easily a customer may purchase a particular team's product. Investments in the distribution network improve a product's accessibility.

Accounting A summary and analysis of the firm's financial position.

Accounts Payable Amount owed to suppliers for raw materials delivered. This value is affected by the number of days taken to pay suppliers (Accounts Payable expressed in days) which may be adjusted on the marketing screen.

Accounts Receivable The amount of money owed to the company by its debtors. This value is affected by both sales volume and our credit policy (accounts receivable lag, expressed in days).

Accumulated Depreciation Cumulative total of each year's depreciation charge for plant and equipment.

Actual Industry Unit Sales Units actually sold into the segment from all products represented. If this value is lower than Available Unit Sales then insufficient units were produced for sale into the segment.

Adjustment for non-cash items Adjustments for income statement transactions, where no cash actually changed hands.

Administration Cost of general administration such as legal services, accounting, and human resources.

Age The preferred perceived age customers would like a product to possess. Perceived age is affected by redesigning (changing the performance attribute, size attribute, or both) the product.

Assets Anything owned by a firm — the organization's "stuff."

Asset Turnover Sales, generated in a particular year, divided by the value of total assets for the same period.

Automation The automation the company will enjoy, on each of its production lines, during the coming round.

B

Balance Sheet Reports the book value of all assets, liabilities, and owner's equity of the firm at a point in time.

Benchmarking A method of evaluating the performance of a business by comparison to some other specified level of accomplishment, typically a level achieved by another company.

Benefits The annual cost of benefits package for each employee.

Board of Directors A set of executives who are responsible for monitoring the activities of the firm's president and other high-level managers, also referred to as the executive management team.

Book Value The amount an asset is valued in business records, not necessarily the same amount as what the asset is worth on the open market.

Bonds Long-term debt securities purchased by investors.

Business Plan A detailed description of a proposed or existing business including the product or services offered, the types of customers it would attract, the competition, and the facilities needed for production.

C

Capacity The straight time capacity the company will enjoy, on each of its production lines, during the coming round.

Cash The amount of cash in the bank.

Cash Flow Statement This statement is published in conformity with the Finance and Accounting Standards Board's (FASB) most recent statements and opinions on the format for a cash flow analysis.

Cash from Long Term Debt Cash received for issuing new, ten-year, bonds is an example of cash generated from long term debt.

Change in Current Assets and Liabilities Items in this category are assets and liabilities that have either increased or decreased since last year's balance sheet. As such the line items either expel or draw in cash.

Change in Current Debt This is the net value of any current debt owed (and therefore had to pay) last year and any additional current debt acquired.

Close The price being paid for the bond in the third party market at the end of the last period. This price is a function of the interest rate and the risk inherent in the security as expressed by its credit rating.

Closing Cash Position Value in the cash account at the end of this year, also shown on the Balance Sheet.

Common Stock Value of monies received for the issuing of stock, since the company's inception (the value of additional paid in capital is included here).

Contribution Margin   Sales revenue less all of the above listed variable costs (and does not include depreciation).

Cumulative Profits   Cumulative total of all profits (losses) generated since the game's inception.

Current Debt   The value of debt owed and payable on January 1st of the year for which decisions are currently being made.

Customer Awareness   That portion of the total segment that was aware of a particular segment.

Customer Survey   This is an assessment of the desirability of a particular product

D

Depreciation   Depreciation an accounting for the portion of the equipment that was effectively "used up" in the period. The government recognizes this wear and tear and allows us to deduct it before declaring a profit. It is added back here to get a true picture of our cash account. Although depreciation is expensed on the income statement, no company check was actually written. Unlike a check for the rent, the cash account never saw a check for depreciation.

Direct Labor   Cost of all labor associated with manufacturing the product. This value may be impacted by raising or lowering the amount of automation (a capital cost) present on a particular line.

Direct Material   Cost of all raw materials necessary to manufacture a product.

Dividends   The income the firm provides to its owners, or shareholders, based on profits.

Dividend's Paid   Value of cash expended on paying dividends. Dividend payment is made on the finance screen and each year defaults to zero unless another value is entered.

E

Earnings Before Interest and Taxes (EBIT)   Net margin less fees and write-offs and bonus income.

Emergency Loan   Amount of cash injected during the year when the company is completely devoid of cash. This is usually a result of inventories building at unexpected levels thus drying up all liquidity. Loans made on an emergency basis have a punitive interest rate (5% above current rate) attached to them.

EPS   EPS is calculated by dividing net profit into the number of shares outstanding.

F

Face Value   The face value of the entire issue. This value is also what would be paid back to the bondholders at the maturity of the debt. However, if bonds are retired (called) early the amount paid may be higher or lower than this.

Fees and Write-offs   This is a compilation of charges that may be incurred during any given period.

G

Gain/Loss on Equipment Sales If machinery is sold at a value that is higher than the net or depreciated value of the machinery, then this shows up as a profit on the income statement. Such gains and losses must be reported on the income statement. However they do not represent a true movement of cash. The cash flow is the total amount received for selling off the line, this amount is shown (net of any purchases) in the cash flows from investing section of the cash flow statement.

Gross Margin Revenue left after deducting direct labor, raw materials and depreciation expressed as a percentage of sales.

Growth Rate Annual compound rate at which unit demand will grow.

I

Income Statement The Income Statement, also known as a Profit and Loss Statement, shows the entire value that an account has accumulated over the previous period (in this case twelve months).

Industry Sales Dollar sales into each segment.

Industry Unit Sales Total units sold by all companies into each segment.

Industry Unit Sales vs. Unit Demand Number of units sold, by all companies, in each segment of the market, versus the number of units demanded. In cases where the units demanded is larger than the units sold, there was an inadequate supply of minimally acceptable product available and thus some demand was unfulfilled.

Inventory Carrying Costs The cost of having inventory in stock.

Inventory Turnover The relationship between the cost of goods sold and inventory calculated by cost of goods sold/inventory.

Inventory Value The value of inventory on hand valued using "average cost accounting". This will rise and fall based on the production scheduled (on the production screen) versus units sold.

L

Labor Cost The per unit cost of labor in the year just ended.

Leverage Total assets at the end of the period under review divided by owners' equity for the same period.

List Price Price charged for the product in the round just ended.

Long Term Debt The value of all outstanding bonds (Ten year) which will become due at some future date.

Long Term Interest Interest paid on outstanding bonds.

M

Market Share Overall percentage share, of the dollar volume, gained each year.

Market Share Actual Market share actually achieved by each product in each segment of the market. The market shares based on units are shown in the left-hand group of columns and the market shares based on dollars are shown in the right-hand group of columns.

Market Share Actual vs. Potential Compares what was sold by a team into a segment with what the team would have sold if they had produced sufficient inventory.

Market Share by Segment Dollar market share of each segment enjoyed by each team.

Market Share Potential This shows the respective market shares each product should have earned if all products had been manufactured in sufficient quantity. In cases where actual share is larger than potential share, then other teams ran out of product and "chased" demand to your inferior product. In cases where potential share is larger than actual, then you stocked out and chased demand to other teams.

Material Cost The per unit cost of direct materials in the year just ended.

Mean Time Between Failure Also referred to as MTBF, this measures the reliability of product expressed in a standard unit of measure, such as in thousands of hours. It is the average time between expected product failures. The longer the duration, or MTBF, the better the product performs.

N

Net Cash from Operations The sub-total of all activities on the cash flow statement to this point. Conceptually it is the actual cash either generated (if positive) or used up (if negative) by the core activities of the business. The remainder of the cash flow statement summarizes activities involved in either capital budgeting or tax and treasury activities.

Net Change in Cash Position The difference between the balance in the cash account at the end of last year and the value of cash account at the end of this year. The entire Cash Flow Statement is designed to reconcile to this value.

Net Income Value of profits as calculated on the income statement.

Net Margin Value of total sales less variable and period costs.

Net Profit Earnings left after all expenses are paid. Net profit can only be allocated to one of two directions. It is either paid out to the owners of the business, in the form of a dividend or it is retained in the business to grow the company and is thus added to the Retained Earnings of the business.

O

Overtime Typically paid at 1.5 times the expected wage, this can also be expressed as the percentage of the production that was undertaken using overtime.

P

Percent of Market   Share of total units sold, represented by each segment of the market.

Perceptual Map   A graph showing marketing information such as a particular segment on the perceptual map and identifies all products that sold 1% or more into that segment.

Period Costs   Costs that generally tend not to move in proportion to sales volume.

Plant Utilization   Volume actually produced during the previous round compared to the actual capacity for that round. For example, levels in excess of 100% indicate overtime was utilized.

Plant and Equipment   Gross value of capacity and automation available (or purchased) for each production line.

Plant Improvements   Net value, after deducting any equipment sold for scrap, of cash invested in automation and capacity.

Positioning   Proximity of product to "sweet spot" within the segment.

Price   Price charged for a product this year.

Price/Earnings Ratio   The closing stock price divided by the earnings per share or EPS. The P/E is sometimes referred to as the earnings multiple or simply the multiple.

Primary Segment   The segment into which the largest proportion of this product was sold.

Production vs. Capacity   Number of units actually built versus the straight time capacity of the entire plant for the year just ended. When production is larger than capacity, overtime must have been scheduled in order to achieve the production level.

Profits   This shows the dollar profit earned each year since the games inception.

Profit Sharing   That share of the profits paid to technicians and assemblers as per the union agreement. (Percentage of profits paid to assemblers and technicians.)

Promotions Budget   Value of monies expended on media advertising, as set on the Marketing screen.

Q

Quality   Desired performance standard of a product or service. This may be measured by MTBF of the product.

R

R&D Costs   Annual costs associated with either redesigning an existing, or designing an entirely new, product. If an R&D project is more than a year in duration, then the cost will be charged out over the full life of the project, with a maximum of one million dollars being charged on a single project, in any given year. For example, if a project is estimated to cost $1.5M then $1M will be charged against this year's Income Statement and $.5M will be charged against next.

Retained Earnings	Total of all company profits and losses of the life of the company, less any dividends paid out. This DOES NOT represent a pile of cash. The monies are captured in the assets of the company. This may be cash but it may just as easily be in the form of plant or even accounts receivable.
Retirement of Long Term Debt	Cash consumed in the early retirement of bonds that are outstanding. These bonds are retired at the value at which they were trading, in the third party market, at the end of the previous year.
Revision Date	The last time product came out of a redesign cycle, in R&D, or the next time it will come out of the redesign cycle if it is currently being redesigned.
ROA	Net profit generated each year, divided by the value of total assets for the same period.
ROE	Net profit generated each year, divided by the value of owners' equity for that year.
ROS	Net profit generated each year, divided by total sales for the same period.

S

S&P	The Standard and Poors' credit rating for additional underwriting of debt for the company ranging from AAA to DDD.
Sales	The value of products sold over the previous twelve months, broken out by product line.
Sales Budget	Monies expended for paying sales personnel and expanding the distribution network. This value is an input on the Marketing screen.
Sales of Common Stock	Value of cash received from the issuing of additional stock. Maximum issue in any year is 20% of the total currently outstanding stock. Stock is issued at its spot prices as of December 31st of the year just ended.
Series Number	The first half of the series number refers to the interest or coupon rate paid on the bonds which are issued in $1000 denominations. The second half of the series number (after the letter "S" which is placed there by convention) refers to the date of maturity, for example a "00" after the "S" would indicate the bond was to mature in the year 2000.
SG&A % Sales	Total of selling general and administrative expenses as a percentage of total sales for that period.
Shares	Number of shares currently outstanding. At the beginning of the game each company has two million shares outstanding.
Short Term Interest	Interest paid on current debt, including interest on emergency loans.
Stock Out	A situation where all products are sold out and it has had a negative effect on sales performance. Thus, it is likely a higher sales level would have been experienced had more units been manufactured and available.

T

Taxes   Taxes paid on income, using a 35% taxation rate.

Total Assets   Total of all current and fixed assets.

Total Available Unit Sales   The actual number of units demanded in the segment under review.

Total Equity   Also known as shareholder equity, owner's equity or net worth. This represents the net value of the company after liabilities are deducted from the value of total assets. The value is calculated by adding, in this case, common stock and retained earnings. This highlights the inherent relationship of the balance sheet. This relationship being owners' equity equals total assets less total liabilities.

Total Fixed Assets   Value of plant and equipment less total accumulated depreciation.

Total Liabilities   Sum total of accounts payable, current debt and long term debt.

Total Period Costs   Accumulation of all period costs described above.

Total Units Demanded   Total units that could have been sold into each segment had sufficient, appropriate product been made available.

U

Units in Inventory   Number of units of the product left in inventory as of December 31st (in 000's of units).

Unit Sales vs. Unit Demand   Number of units our company sold, in each segment of the market, versus the number of units that segment wished to purchase from our company. In cases where the units demanded is greater than units sold, we did not build sufficient product and thus stocked out. In cases where units demanded are less than units sold, other teams stocked out and pushed demand to us that our product did not "deserve". However as our product was minimally acceptable, it was begrudgingly purchased by the market.

Units' Sold   The total number of this product sold into all market segments.

V

Variable Costs   Costs that vary in direct proportion to the number of units sold.

W

Wage Escalator   Annual cost of living adjustment applied to assemblers and technicians hourly wages.

Y

Yield   Dividend payment as a percentage value of the closing stock price, or the interest paid on the bond divided by the actual trading price of the bond.

Index